GROWING THROUGH GRIEF

The Alchemy of Healing From Loss

By Michele Mariscal

Copyrights

Contents

Introduction

———— · ✱ · ————

Grief shows itself in mysterious ways, hidden in your emotional and mental bodies, affecting your physical body and making itself known when it asks to be tended. This past year when my big brother Michael died, I thought I was moving through my grief and handling my emotions and getting back to my life as I used to know it. After all, I had experienced many losses in my life and I knew how this went. What I didn't take into consideration was the compounding effects of several losses all piled into a span of a year and a half.

Not only had my dad just died when my brother received his diagnosis of stage 4 esophageal cancer, but my own health had become demanding in ways that exponentially increased the stress I was experiencing. I had been an athlete for 30 years and relied on exercise as therapy and stress relief. But over the past two years I had been dealing with back pain from degeneration, and also had a tear in the cartilage in my hip that had worsened to the point where I couldn't walk without pain. I was also smack in the middle of menopause, dealing with the changes it brought to my body. This was a LOT of loss at once.

The fact that I had become fairly non-functional in my life was not apparent to me until I started making some blaring mistakes. To name a big one, I booked a flight to see my family when I already had those dates booked with business travel. I had no working memory of making any plans, nor did I seem to be able to use my calendar! Somehow the digital world of calendars on devices didn't register for me. It was like a world of the invisible that I couldn't see and I needed to go back to using a pencil and paper calendar.

I also did not understand I had begun to isolate myself in an unhealthy way. I kept passing it off as my need to retreat to my introverted self to gather some energy. I didn't realize I had so very little energy to be with people to begin with! I thought I had developed an ability to move through grief because of all the past experiences I had, like the sheer knowledge that I had done this many times before should have made adjusting to loss in my life easier this time—but it didn't. Grief is cumulative.

I am sure I'm not alone in this. There are many people— probably some of you who are reading this book—in the situation I was in, who recognize a need to tend to grief. I also think many more people have buried their grief experience, unprocessed, and it shows up in different ways and at different times, sometimes unearthed under the guise of some other emotional drama. There are so many ways that grievers avoid feeling pain. It is so much easier to seek out distractions and do other things like shop, binge Netflix, drink, gamble, or any other number of over-indulging activities to push away what lies deeply buried.

Through many of my own bouts with anger, I've recognized that some expression of sadness lies underneath. In one recent experience, I had a day I just called "crabby," but after my third explosive anger reaction, I found a place in the office where I could be alone and just started crying. As I kept letting the tears flow the sadness became overwhelming, and I realized I was approaching the one-year anniversary of my brother's death. The days leading up to his death had been so painful, and the memories were resurfacing unbeknownst to me. I had no idea I was remembering and processing this sadness on any conscious level, but my emotional and spiritual body knew. In my head and on the calendar I was aware of it, but I didn't know I needed to express the emotions of it—until I did. When my tears stopped I felt clear and could go on with my day. What arose after I allowed myself to express this sadness were thoughts of my family and my love for them, my appreciation for my workplace that has supported me through numerous difficult years of several losses, and the acknowledgement of myself seeking love above all else.

Grief and loss offer two distinct paths—one of continued sadness, bitterness, regret, guilt, and shame—or one of love and seeking the capacity to love more. The possibility of learning about yourself as a loving being is what lies beyond the intense experience of loss. A part of you is dying in this process and what awaits is the rebirth of something new. Unless you do the work of allowing and experiencing this loss, what is there to be birthed in you continues to wait.

In the midst of grief, when I first experienced it after the death of my little brother Martin in 1993, I wrote this journal excerpt that would set the stage for how I handled the many losses that would come over the twenty-five years following my first intense loss in life: "To sit and feel the pain again is hard, and yet through the greatest pain has come the greatest love in my life. As we cleared away his (Martin's) belongings, I felt how temporary everything seemed, but not the love. It endures and can't be put away. And so I try to go on with all of it and remember that all of me except the love is also temporary."

This book is about my personal journey, as well as the journey of others who shared their story of grief and loss with me, and how they are moving forward. In its pages are suggestions, inspirations, and exercises to help you process grief and work toward healing, knowing you are not alone.

Chapter 1

My Story, Thoughts, and Perspectives

——— · ✦ · ———

I came to a point recently in my life when I realized I was suffering a very mild case of PTSD. Even describing it that way signifies that I was—and still am, in some ways—in denial about grief in my life. Have you noticed how our culture has to categorize and give a label to our states of disease? What was really there was a whole pile of thoughts and emotions that still needed to be expressed. When you are a high-achieving, high-functioning person and grief enters your life, it can't be "handled" like everything else that you do so highly functioning! It can be messy and confusing and so difficult that the mere act of making the decision between the choice of salmon or chili for dinner is impossible. I was there not so many months ago when I first started writing this book. I had to cancel the remodel of a bathroom in my home because I couldn't fathom having to make all the decisions that needed to be made, choices about fixtures, and cabinetry, and colors....when really, I didn't care.

In the process of writing this book I spoke with about 25 people who have experienced, or were in the midst of experiencing, grief and loss of a loved one. Their stories and reflections are included throughout this book.

Grief as a Process in Life

Grief is, perhaps, the most under-expressed and under-experienced emotion in human lives until it strikes in a sudden, or pending, loss.

When a death of a loved one occurs it has a finality to it that feels as though part of you has been lost forever. The shock and numbness in the first days and weeks give way to any number of feelings. A short list includes sorrow, misery, sadness, anguish, pain, distress, heartache, heartbreak, agony, torment, affliction, suffering, woe, desolation, dejection, and despair. Initially there may be support from those around you to move through days and weeks after a loss, but eventually a new sense of life without your loved one must be found.

And then there are the myriad of other kinds of grief that are passed over routinely. There are over forty types of loss. In this book I am focusing primarily on the death of loved ones, but as I shared in the introduction, other losses impact the experience of losing someone. Grief has a cumulative effect on your whole picture of loss, which may include divorce or a break-up, the loss of a pet, the loss of a career, or bankruptcy, to name a few. All loss adds to what you are holding in you. Every transition in life brings some amount of grief with it, which is rarely expressed. It is back to school time as I work on this book and I see the transitions of children going to school for the first time and those leaving home and going off to college. People are experiencing great joy and sadness in the same moment. Being fully with both of these emotions and sharing that with those involved is so good and makes life rich! Working with emotions and sharing them out loud with one another seems to be the missing part—we do not do that well for so many different reasons in our cultures, in our families, even in our own head!

Some of my own transitions at the moment include moving through the gate of menopause and the changes that brings to my body, as well as dealing with injuries that have made it very difficult for me to be the athlete I have been for 30 years. I think these things combined with the loss of my dad and Michael, my older brother, compounded the effects that led to a mild case of PTSD. I would not have described it as that at the time—PTSD is what people who have been severely traumatized experience. But one of my doctors explained to me that being in chronic pain (from my injuries) and having back-to-back losses is traumatizing, too. In my high-achieving, logical-minded way I was just trying to push through it all. I had suffered grief many times before and thought I was doing what I needed to do in order to process it. But this time was different and I felt like the twenty-five years since the devastating loss of my little brother Martin had all begun to surface for me.

It was like I had this container, or cauldron, of loss to contend with and it flattened me in my life. I felt as though I was traveling on two different timelines, one in which I showed up to work every day, and the other in which I was processing massive amounts of memories and being with each of them until I had experienced and moved through to the other side. It made life difficult, and yet I felt a sacredness to the whole thing. I remember reading parts of *The Red Book*, the personal journal and writings of Carl Jung, which outlined what he described as his "confrontation with the unconscious." My journey felt like a hint of that kind of experience.

Models of Grief from the Clinical Realm

There are many models of the stages of grief, which can be helpful in describing emotional states we may experience when dealing with loss. While some people may look at these stages as distinct and time-bound, the reality is that they can be experienced in any order and may recur at any time. They provide a framework for the intellectual part of you that seeks some meaning through information. I provide it here because often people have to start where we usually live—inside our head.

Here are some of the frameworks that have been proposed. Remember that loss is not a cookie cutter journey, and no two people experience grief in the same way.

1. **Kubler-Ross Model** — In the work of Swiss-American psychiatrist Elisabeth Kubler-Ross, the five stages of grief are: denial, anger, bargaining, depression, and acceptance. The Kubler-Ross Model was originally intended to help those facing the reality of their own death. It quickly became utilized by practitioners for the analysis and treatment of grieving individuals. The model and the five stages of grief can be found in the mainstream media applied to anything from divorce to global markets. While this model shows a continuum of emotions that a griever may go through, I think it can be challenging if the expectation is that you will go through these exact stages in this order. Each experience of grief is unique and individual. As her career progressed, Kubler-Ross worked much more in the spiritual domain of the human being in the experience of dying and bringing solace to those left to grieve the loss of a loved one.

2. **Lindemann's Model** — In the 1940s, German-American author and psychiatrist Erich Lindemann provided some of the earliest research revealing the long-term impact of grief and trauma. His body of work brought to the field an understanding of the symptomology of grief. He provided the evidence that grief is not just psychological but also has a physical impact. To this day,

his findings provide a deeper basis for developing ways to do "grief work" in our culture as a part of our health and wellness practices.

3. **Four Tasks of Grief Model** — Psychologist William Worden's Four Tasks of Grief model suggests that for the process of mourning to be completed, there are four tasks one must accomplish. Worden also acknowledges that grief is not linear and some tasks may need to be repeated.

Again, these models can provide some comfort that what you are going through is normal and known and studied. There is a universality to the experience, but it is *your* story and you will live it in whatever order and fashion is right and true for you.

Spiritual and Cultural Thoughts on Grief and Loss

In my experience, grief is a deep journey of the Soul, happening at a level that challenges you to experience not only the physical experience of loss, but also the more existential reality that death and rebirth are two sides of the same coin. Your Soul knows this. Your brain can only embrace the words until you connect your heart and Soul in the experience you are having. It is an opportunity for growth unlike any other in life. I can take this view now, but I understand if you just had a flinch of confusion and possibly even disdain. Many spiritual traditions speak of human struggle as initiation into growing further into your spiritual nature. I find this concept more life-giving than the view of avoiding suffering at all costs. If you are deep in your grieving process right now, these words may not have much meaning but I hope that you can feel a potential for something good to come. Some of the stories of other people's journeys through grief in this book may help illustrate that for you.

Alchemists describe processes that allow you to discover and take up the impulse that is found in the alchemical "ash." What you are depositing in your grief is ash that holds a seed for something else to come. The activities that help create flexibility of soul (more about this in later chapters) provide forward movement and discovery, rather than stagnation and lethargy in life. Stay awake to what is happening in the darkness. Are you developing new eyes to see something in a new way? Are people showing up in your life and bringing some light to your darkness?

Culturally, we as Americans do not live in a society that embraces ritual, ceremony, or healing ways in death and loss, or grief. There is, however, a growing movement in communities that assists people with conscious dying. I think this will help in matters of grief and support for those who feel the loss and are adjusting to life without a loved one. Indigenous cultures have communal structures and understandings that vastly differ from our isolationist ways of dealing with grief. Many cultures have the understanding that if one person is not well in the village, the whole village is not well. Feelings of grief not expressed, experienced, or prepared for in some reverent way can lead to states of depression and anxiety and even post-traumatic stress. The draw to numb and drown and silence the pain is intense. While short bouts of numbing in some ways may seem to help you deal with the grief, the danger is in getting lost in the unconsciousness of sadness.

The primary need to successfully continue to move through grief is awareness and movement of emotions as they occur for as long as they occur. In western cultures the mindset of finding solutions and fixing what is wrong compounds the ability to experience grief in a way that brings growth. This "fix it" mindset can be detrimental to what is healing and helpful. Being able to face, feel, and experience sadness and grief fully is necessary to move forward, again and again and again in some instances. Facing your fear of stepping into these emotions is needed. You may be afraid of the unknown, afraid your tears will never stop, afraid you will forget your loved one, afraid you will lose yourself. None of these things are easy to face! But you must do so in order to move forward.

Part of grief must be done in aloneness, for it is you who must adjust and adapt to newness without your loved one, but community is also an important aspect of the grief process. Individual inner work brings great reward, but it is important to recognize if you are seeking aloneness to isolate yourself, or to develop deeper movement in your own grief and a deeper spiritual connection to this process.

Grief, loss, and continued sadness can create a state of being that one might describe as a dullness of life, or worse, an inability to engage in a meaningful way in one's life. In spiritual traditions, periods of this nature are called "the dark night of the soul" and are generally accepted to be an inherent aspect of spiritual growth. Seeing a spiritual perspective, staying awake to what is growing, and seeing what is new brings hope to even the darkest days. Many find that nature is healing and brings comfort. When you look to the world of nature with spiritual eyes, you can meditate on the growth of a flower and see all of life and death as a process. While you are not a plant, exercises such as these bring recognition that you are a part of the natural world. They also help with the understanding that grief is a universal experience, part of a larger world of death and rebirth. Questions like "Why am I here?" and "What is my life for?" often drive a quest for explanation and exploration that leads to deeper spiritual understanding. These questions often surface in the face of grief and loss.

Grief Can Take its Toll in Different Ways

There may be many well-intentioned people who say things like, "It's time to move on" or, "just stay busy." Yet grief is not something to move on from without fully acknowledging and processing it. What does need to happen is finding movement forward in life with this loss now a part of your identity. It is here that a choice lies— either you lean into the loss with an attitude to understand what new possibilities may be arising, what rebirth is being offered, or you stay stuck. Seeing that this choice exists is a first step. There are some, however, who cannot tolerate being in the conversation of loss any longer and wish to move past it; they want something else out of the relationship. Grief and loss may bring new people into your life, but it oftentimes ushers others out.

This in itself can bring more grief, but if you stay awake to what is happening you may learn more about yourself and the steps forward that are being offered in subtle ways. There may be others who come into your life at this time who become important to you. There may be qualities that you find you are strengthening in yourself. If you use the framework and question, "What is being birthed?" it is an opportunity to see all of what is happening and not remain fixated on your loss.

Grief and loss are shared human experiences but are often missing components of health and wellness activities in this culture. Untended and unexpressed grief and loss stored in the body often resurface in a crisis of health. Massage therapists speak about pockets of emotion that are released when working on a certain area of the body. Medical intuitives speak of mapping particular emotions and beliefs to places in the body. I studied with Carol Ritberger PhD, a medical intuitive, for 10 years from 2002-2012 as part of my development to do spiritual healing work for others. Through studying with her, I learned that grief and loss are mapped to the lungs, and often in my work as a spiritual healer I found pockets of grief in the lungs that needed to be dislodged and experienced and expressed. Cases of chronic, complicated grief—in which the individual is unable to be with the loss that has taken place—occur in about 10% of individuals. Processing grief can be made more difficult by well-meaning friends and family who put a time limit or inflict personal opinions about how you are grieving. It is important, though, to recognize if/when you have moved into a state in which you can no longer engage in life in meaningful ways, when your attempts to find purpose after your loss have not brought comfort. Grief is not a cookie-cutter journey and each person is unique. Each loss is unique as well and will bring different levels of experience and teaching.

Loss and illness are often a call from the Spirit, a call to enter more deeply into the Mystery. There are a myriad of ways that people find and respond to this call. In the years when I worked actively as a shamanic practitioner, many of those who came to my healing sessions were suffering from some kind of grief. For grief in particular, some of the ceremonies and rituals brought solace and some hope of a solid footing. Ceremonies done in community, such as a "Spirit Canoe," provide an experience of conversation and releasing of any attachments still held with a loved one. (I will describe this more in detail later in the book). It is often this attachment, this not letting go, that brings continual pain. Recognizing this helps you find ways to see the connection to your loved one still exists; it just exists in a different form.

When my little brother died I was deep in the study of molecular biology. At the time, I could readily accept this concept from physics that energy in a closed system never dies; rather, it is transformed from one form to another. For a while this helped me cope with my grief, but in time I began to ask questions about why he died, and thus my deep dive into learning about soul families, soul contracts, and soul journey began. The physical part of you may be given by measurements of frequency and electromagnetic energy, but the essential self has more to do with a connection to higher energy, a Qi, or Chi as spoken of in many cultures. It is a spiritual element in our physical nature that works in tandem with a mechanical energy.

Having flexibility of Soul helps us move with emotional flexibility. Practices that provide this are expressive in art, movement, and written word. Anytime you can express what is inside of you in a way that provides an image of what you are feeling, you are creating movement. For example, art therapy can be a useful tool and people are often surprised at what comes out of themselves. When you take steps to do something, you move your sadness just a little (or maybe a lot!).

My own journey with grief has spanned 25 years and on some days I have been terrified the well of sadness was so deep that I will never climb out of it, or wondered if there even is a way to ascend. It was shocking when I realized years had gone by and still I would be confronted by these feelings that welled up and would not move until I made some choice to either just be with them or take some action that lifted me out. The key was to recognize these moments as my old friend grief and then take some action.

Emotions of this kind are not easily experienced, and most of us are not taught how to express them. In fact, in much of my upbringing I was told to *not* experience them, or if I did, not for very long. My own journey took me deep into darkness and sadness, but as I grew and learned more about myself as a spiritual being, I took the perspective that my grief experience was building something in me spiritually. I lifted myself and was able to choose to be engaged in life and process grief at every turn of a reminder or memory of the one I lost. I was creating newness in myself that I would not understand until much later. Building a resilience and understanding has allowed me to face fears over and over again with each person I have lost in my life.

Sometimes the only way out…is in.

Chapter 2

Wrapping My Head Around Grief

———— · ✿ · ————

When I was thirty-one I moved to San Francisco and started school at U.C. Berkeley to finish my bachelor's degree. During the first semester my little brother became very ill around Thanksgiving and on December 9, 1992 was diagnosed with Acute Lymphocytic Leukemia. He died on February 17, 1993. There was such hope for a cure because of his age and strength and positive attitude, but that was his time to leave this life on Earth. It was completely devastating, shocking, and unimaginable, and I felt so many things at once after he died. I did not know how to handle the depth of sadness that all of us in my family and his girlfriend experienced.

I studied and searched and read as much as I could about grief as I was moving through my first experience of losing a loved one. I found that reading through the models and stages of grief helped ease my brain a little. During the initial phase of grief, I just needed to know that some of the things I was experiencing were normal. You may be having this question too—am I normal?? At some point the words began to blur together for me as my emotions continued on a rollercoaster. Learning that an array of emotions could be felt, that there can be several stages and several tasks to this grief journey, helped me.

This did not last long, though. The knowledge provided information but I found I was thrown into an irrational, non-linear, non-logical world...and you may be feeling that way, too.

Recognize that your journey of getting through *your* grief may take on its own path that might include all of the emotions included in different models, or it might not. You may enter some stages and stay there for quite some time. Your path may move fast, or slow, and not include all the stages in any given framework. Later on in this book I will introduce you to an exercise designed to help you work with your emotions and see movement in them. Rather than think you need to fit into some sequence, working with your emotions rather than just reading about them will help you move in your own time and discover what is yours to learn and experience.

The most important thing is to acknowledge, express, and keep moving through your own journey. See your grief as a continuous process. Some cases of grief feel monumental, such as losing a loved one to a violent crime, losing a child suddenly, losing someone to suicide, or losing a life-long partner. The work of grief as it moves into adjusting to loss is to establish how you move forward, what you learn, what you find anew in your life, and how you grow out of this tragedy.

Often, individuals can feel so lost without the person who has died that they lose sight of their own worth. It can be difficult to feel why life matters at all without the one who is no longer here. But I'm here to tell you there *is* hope, and your life matters.

How Grief Feels

During the couple years leading up to my mother's death in 2010, I found myself grieving as her neurological disease progressed. I felt guilty for not being able to be with her more because I lived in California and she and my dad lived in Washington. Then when I did visit I was so overwhelmingly sad to see the changes happening. And then I felt guilty for the relief I felt being able to go home. During this period of time I met and befriended someone whom I desperately wanted to be in a relationship with but could not because he was married. I'm sure that my neediness to have someone by my side to console me through this grief with my mother was driving all sorts of dysfunctional emotions. At the time I was just trying to cope. This combination of longing and pining after someone for several years in this very dysfunctional way, along with the grief I experienced when my mother died, created a compounded loss effect that took me into a very dark place. When I look back on my life during that period of time, it shocks me to see the depths of isolation I fell into.

Here is a snapshot of what days in my life looked like back then, a typical scenario that became many, many weeks on end during this dark period:

I prepared my food to take to work the following day— another Monday—and looked out my kitchen window at the cars parked in the carport. I hadn't moved my car since Friday evening when I got home from work. I also had not taken a shower all weekend. Somehow I just didn't care. I went out on the river trail very early on Saturday and Sunday so I wouldn't have to see or meet happy people later in the day, who would expect a response to their cheerful hello. I took the recycling box in my house out to the bin in the carport and listened to the hard clank of wine bottles as they tumbled into the can. I shopped at 8am for groceries so that I could be in and out of the store before the world became busy with people.

When Monday morning came, I finally dragged myself out of bed. My shower felt cleansing and I wanted to stay in it as I broke down in sobbing tears again. Somehow it felt safe to let go of what I had stored up and avoided over the weekend. I braced myself for work, put eye drops in my eyes and concealer under my eyes. I prepared my outer self for the world and pushed my grief back into its hidden inner place.

Grief can be overwhelming and seemingly unending. Trying to manage life when you have to return to work or other responsibilities can make you feel like you are split in two. I was fortunate (notice how after all of these years I can see the positive in the situation!) to be able to withdraw from school for a semester and leave my part time jobs for a month when my little brother Martin died in 1993. I spent a month with my mom and dad on the east coast. When I did return to school, however, the rigor of study and competition often pushed me to tears. I had a whole new situation that I had to adjust to in my grief. What helped me most then was lots and lots of exercise and finding a counselor on campus I could meet with once a week. I trained myself to save up these emotions and go into his office and cry for an hour. It was so helpful to know someone was there for me to express this. It normalized grief for me in an environment where I could not express it. At U.C. Berkeley the name of the game was excel! I didn't feel I had support in my inner life of turmoil in any other place but my counselor's office. He gave me things to do when I was not in school, which helped to keep things moving over the weekend.

I wasn't sure my brain was ever going to engage again at the level I needed it to with the pre-med studies I was doing. It felt overwhelming, and at times I tried to stuff what I was feeling away just so that I could keep studying. Eventually these emotions came out in one way or another—some not the healthiest (i.e. drinking alcohol). I made allowances just to get through but I could feel my inner turmoil brewing.

Really hard questions were surfacing, like, what is life for if you work as hard as he did in school and take the bar exam, become a lawyer, and then just end up dying? What is my life for and why am I working so hard? What difference does life make?! These questions were at a level of spiritual understanding that I didn't feel I had answers for from my religious upbringing. In fact, the concept of living a good life in order to go to heaven and having one life with which to fulfill this task didn't make any sense to me at all. I had already stopped going to mass on a regular basis because I could not be in alignment with some of the church doctrine. Love, unconditional love in the way that I thought about it, seemed to encompass a different kind of empathy and compassion for ALL humans than I was asked to practice. This was my perception at the time and I do not mean to judge anyone in their path or beliefs. I think we each seek alignment with our own truth and at the heart of it all we move toward love. I did miss the deep sense of community that my church participation had always offered, though, and I wondered how I was going to find it again. I could feel that this grief experience had some requirement of community and shared stories and tears in order to get through it. At that time, my community became my school and the gym.

Thankfully, exercise is very beneficial in stabilizing the

hormonal mush that floods your body while you're grieving. The stress hormones released in grief can be part of the compounding problem that can lead to anxiety and depression if not addressed. Finding ways to manage this stress on the nervous system and hormonal system helps. Many forms of yoga, breathing practices, and all sorts of exercise in general are beneficial for this purpose. In fact, just getting yourself up off the couch or out of bed and making really big arm circles or doing some squats can kick-start you on a bad day. I know to some of you this may sound too simplistic, but by making any small choice to move something (a thought, an emotion, a body part) you are building what will become your greatest ally in this struggle—your will and your power to make a choice.

Loss to Suicide

A couple years later as I was adjusting to life without my little brother, two of my friends from high school committed suicide a week apart from each other. I did not have many friends who had known me in my younger years because we moved often as a military family. These two friendships were meaningful to me. The first was a friend who had been dealing with alcoholism since high school. My friend's business partner had called me from Atlanta where they had gone to see the Olympics that year. He said he didn't know what to do with her and asked if I would fly out to take her back home and check her into a hospital and hopefully get her into rehab. I had not seen her for a couple of years and it was heart-wrenching to see this vibrant, beautiful woman in the state she was in.

I stayed with her until they stabilized her in the hospital. Her liver was severely damaged. The next step was rehab, which was being set up, so I flew home to California at that point. I got the call the next day that she had taken the rest of the bottle of Tylenol she had in her purse and died quickly from the overdose and the load on her liver.

After flying back up for the funeral and returning home, I just wanted to crawl into a hole and be alone for a while. A couple days after I got home, the second suicide happened. I got a call from the mom of my first boyfriend—whom over the years I'd maintained a friendship with—to let me know he had shot himself. I got back on a plane and flew to Seattle, Washington again for another funeral. I felt like I was on some kind of autopilot, totally numb.

I faced one more loss in that five-year span—my running buddy, who had gotten pregnant with her first child at age 37, died in childbirth. She had undiagnosed fibroid tumors at the time she became pregnant. During childbirth they caused so much bleeding along with birthing her baby boy that she bled out. I could not even attend her funeral I was so turned upside down. The compounding effects of these grief experiences were just too much for me.

Losing More Family

The more recent losses took me yet again into deep grief. Going through Dad's things when he died around Christmas in 2015 was difficult because it included some of the things he and Mom had shared together, and they'd died within a few years of each other. The years after Mom died in 2010 had been filled with care and concern for Dad as he became more and more lonely. The eventual decision to sell their (his) house was difficult but he did see that he needed to be around more people. The location he moved into was a beautiful environment and full of military veterans with whom he could tell stories and have bonding conversations with about their lives. His independent apartment had been stuffed with too many boxes that never got unpacked in the two years he lived there. He could not part with everything when we moved him out of the house and then did not have the space to pull things out of the boxes. Many of them were photographs and photo albums. It's painful going through and throwing away your parents' memories, and holding on to some that were part of your life together. And now there is not much opportunity to talk about those memories with anyone who remembers.

I had this sinking realization that this is how it goes: you live, you consume and stockpile lots of stuff with memories, then you die and you have to go through it all and throw it away, give it away, or stockpile it in your own home as a memory. Having moved Dad out of the house, we had thrown lots of things away and donated many others, so this was the third time with my parents' belongings. At some point again on that trip it was just too much to handle. His funeral was two days before Christmas and to add to the sadness very few people were able to attend his funeral. My dad, who had lived as a charming, gregarious person whom people loved to be around because he found the happy in any situation, scarcely had fifty people at his funeral. I don't know why that made me so sad but it still does if I think about it too much.

My two brothers and I lived in three different states and planned a family trip to be together in Washington. In July that year we had a wonderful vacation, just being together, and I remember thinking, okay, this is our little family now. A couple months later, in November, my older brother Michael received a Stage 4 terminal esophageal cancer diagnosis. I felt the breath leave my lungs and wasn't sure I could take the next breath in—this couldn't be happening. I heard myself repeating over and over to myself, "It's too much, it's just too much, we haven't even closed Dad's estate."

This part of the journey now included adjusting to almost all of my family being gone. There was only my younger brother and I left out of a family of six and this time, unlike all the others, I was feeling my own mortality. For a number of months I felt like I was dangling, unhinged, unrooted, and unanchored. That has subsided as I have taken up the work to serve others through their grief and loss.

A Way Forward

Many people report some kind of communication with their loved one after dying. My dad told me he consistently talked with Mom after she died and he heard her speaking back to him, often as he was going to sleep or coming out of sleep. My own increased intuitive experiences became very apparent to me all those years ago, even as my little brother Martin was going through the two and a half months of treatment. I was alone in my car on the drive back and forth from San Francisco to Stanford Medical Center every day. Something was awakening in me that I could perceive on a very subtle level as I drove in silence most days. There was some kind of shimmering beauty that was opening amidst the massive amount of pain I was experiencing. After Martin's death this sense of "other" experience set me on a path of exploration of many spiritual studies for the next fifteen years. It helped me to understand this journey with grief as part of my own soul and another soul's path together.

Within these years in between my younger brother's death and my older brother's death, I studied and communed with Spirit in a way that opened my heart to see that a heart does not break apart—it breaks open. It is out of this breaking open that newness emerges. The Irish poet and

25

philosopher John O'Donohue spoke of this potential, of this birth through the heart. Everything that happens to you has the potential to deepen you. Each experience is a birth to that potential. Do you have the courage to feel the depth of your grief? There is great potential in falling all the way into your grief in a supported way, surrendering to this idea that you are birthing something in yourself in the process.

When my perspective changed, my habits of thought changed. When my understanding changed, my actions changed.

As I began to see and live the reality that at the moment of birth, we begin a process of moving towards death, it made me think and feel differently. My quest for meaning took me into searching for and learning and experiencing many spiritual teachings and forms of spiritual healing.

I remember my first bout of anger came days after my little brother died and my anger was about praying. I was so angry that we had prayed for an outcome *we* wanted when what would have served me better was to pray for wisdom. In retrospect, this thought was quite a high level thought in a moment of such intense anger, and I took it to heart. I now have an understanding and pray for the highest good for all involved, which may or may not be what I want it to be. There is a spiritual hygienic nature to this allowing for things to unfold with grace and support for all involved. Death is a part of life and the more I am able to allow and recognize and love all that is given in a situation, the more agile and emotionally flexible I become. Still, however, there are the human emotional attachments and regrets and sadness that are mine to work through. This is a part of the work.

There is Hope

Emotional agility is a skill that can be learned and is very important in the grief process. As a speaker and trainer in workplace wellness, I have seen the flood of work in this direction in the last ten years. Mindfulness, meditation, and positive psychology have all become a part of the fabric of professional development to prepare leaders to be better leaders through increased emotional agility, and to help teams perform better together. Thankfully these skills are all helpful in personal as well as professional life. Sadly, it is not uncommon for whole workplaces to need crisis intervention assistance following mass shooting at schools and workplaces.

My years of experience with the work from the Institute of HeartMath® were a saving grace in these last few years. This organization has been doing research for nearly 20 years on the effect of emotions on our cognitive abilities, resilience, and performance. Some of their original research in the 1990s established the understanding that emotions are faster than thought and that becoming aware of your heart through focused breathing and choosing a renewing emotion changes your physiology. Their work and research spans many disciplines and industries. Their many techniques and technology have helped millions to learn how to regulate emotions to attain a more resilient life. One of the techniques is called Notice and Ease. Being able to move in a state of "ease" and heart-centered awareness continuously as I visited my older brother's family every few weeks was so helpful. It helped me be there for my brother Michael in a way that was for him, not for me, even though it was hard. As much as I wanted to talk about the realities of the situation and prepare and talk about dying, he did not. I was able to stay in compassion and not inflict on him what I wanted to talk about. It was difficult for me to do, but I knew it was what he wanted and needed.

My days are lived in balance now with memories taking me into sadness at times, but I am also able to see that having such an experience with my loved ones brought great joy. So I choose the joy! As I mentioned earlier, the power of choice and asserting your will to choose is your greatest tool. You may be feeling hopeless and stuck in grief and unable to make peace with death. That is what this book is about. It is for you. Keep reading and you will find some tools that can help you in your movement forward.

Chapter 3

Grief is Universal But Each Experience is Unique

————— · ✴ · —————

Each Time is Unique

What I have learned about grief is that every situation is unique. Each of the losses I have experienced over the last 25 years held different work for me to do; each challenged me in different ways. Each time I had to grapple with my identity, sometimes being challenged by a sense of my own mortality, which can be really uncomfortable the first time the recognition of your own death is in your face. Regret, guilt, and shame are all emotions that are part of the process, but love, empathy, joy, connectedness, and care are all emotions that counteract these negative emotions. Grief may bring feelings of isolation and aloneness that compound the difficult emotions. An important thing to remember is that grief is a universal experience, a universal emotion felt by everyone at some point. It can be helpful to remember as you move in your own path of grief.

Whether you choose to process with others or to walk your path on a more individual basis, it is a journey and a process. It is helpful to find others who are processing a similar grief experience. There are many different kinds of grief and those who have lost loved ones to violence or suicide take a different path than those moving through a very difficult relationship breakup. Groups that have a common experience can help with the aloneness and isolation that grieving people often feel. I found that I did not want to be in a grief group, but meeting with a counselor for a while was very helpful.

An important step in your journey is to recognize when you are spinning a web so dense that you can't get out of it. The problem is it can be difficult to see when you are there. Others around you may have opinions about where you should be in your life following your loss. It can be alienating when people say to you, "Isn't it time to move forward or move on?" When you don't feel like you can, nor do you have any access to forward movement, this kind of advice or counsel from well-meaning friends is difficult. The word "happy" may not seem to exist in your vocabulary. States of joy might seem unachievable and foreign, like you will never feel joy again.

After my older brother Michael passed away (some months ago now) I was thrown into so many family memories that brought such pain I attempted to escape on some days through eating lots of food and drinking lots of wine. I had been an athlete for 30 years but had sustained back and hip injuries that were taking painfully long to heal. I was grieving this loss of physical ability and it hadn't occurred to me the toll it was taking. I had lost my "go to" way of dealing with everything stressful. My default when I wasn't managing my stress well was sugar bingeing, which now had reached a scary level. I could feel the draw of bulimia, which I'd had a brief brush with in my twenties. I added that to the bag of grief that I carried around with me and did what I could to move, because not moving was not an option. I knew I had to address this addictive part of me that was turning to sugar and flour to bring some calm to my body.

Facing Emotions

Thankfully, during this time I found Bright Line Eating, a program that provided a missing piece in all of my education and training on nutrition, diets, and weight management. In Bright Line Eating, I learned about the neuroscience of addiction to sugar and flour and the differing levels of susceptibility based on an individual's neural pathways. I am high on the susceptibility scale for this addiction, which was not a surprise to me, but I had not found the tools to deal with it. Mindful and intuitive eating doesn't work for a sugar addict. Some may back away from a label as an "addict," but it has given me a framework that makes sense to me and helps me change my habits around the addictive qualities in my eating habits.

I started dealing with the part of myself that wanted to control everything, the part that wanted to "handle" grief. As part of this work I had to start facing my emotions head-on as I was changing my habits around eating. Since I couldn't manage my sugar binges with marathon amounts of running anymore, I felt like I had found the tools and community to support this part of my life. I continue to be a part of the community and work continuously to stay on plan and heal my neural pathways of addiction.

It felt overwhelming to be trying to change my habits with food, but it also was a process that went right along with the inner work I was doing with grief. It's a tricky thing to develop the practice of experiencing what you are feeling and move in tough emotions and then make sure you're not stopping there and stepping into quicksand. Support, support, support helps! I think the unique thing about the Bright Line Eating community is just that—community is built and encouraged and cultivated. I'm spending time on this topic because many times grievers turn to something, anything, to *not* feel what needs to be felt. I found others in the community who were also experiencing grief, and having calls and conversations with them was helpful.

My grief required me to stop, to be with, and to choose how I was going to move. Downward or upward? Each time I found myself spiraling downward, I had the opportunity to strengthen myself in some way by making a choice to be more than the sadness I felt. All of the actions I took were steps in my healing path forward. Sometimes the most healing thing I did in the day was cry until I felt I could not cry any longer. The tears seemed to release something out of me that created an opening for something new.

By this time I had been practicing the techniques from HeartMath®, such as the Notice and Ease method I mentioned earlier, and this shift in emotions was familiar to me as a habit. The different techniques always start with focusing on your heart, which provides for a different energy than just staying in your head. When you are in grief it is difficult to move into anything that feels remotely happy, but it is beneficial to know that emotions like compassion and empathy shift your physiology. These emotions are extremely helpful. They shift what is happening at the level of your nervous system and change the flow of hormones your body is experiencing. This can impact your ability to sleep better, which is typically very difficult in times of grief. I think these practices of HeartMath® are so valuable in building the habit of being with your emotions and noticing where you are at any given time. This ability to choose and shift is very healing in grief. It may be for now that you move into compassion, choosing compassion for yourself first. Then, as you begin to connect with others and do grief work together, you may access and express compassion and empathy for others.

Another step into my recovery from deep long-lasting grief came in the form of a speaking engagement. I was on a stage in front of a few hundred wellness professionals, giving a short speech about my wellness story. I shared a brief part of my challenges with grief, which at the moment was overwhelming me. I challenged my audience to pay attention, to make sure that people were not falling through the cracks in our workplaces without the support they need. I have a tremendously supportive workplace and I work in wellness, and I was slipping below the water line. I made an appeal to my audience that we observe and pay attention to others around us to recognize when another may be in need. This was a group of worksite wellness people, so the appeal was in line with other initiatives speakers were sharing about that day.

This act of being vulnerable and sharing my story was a turning point. I had planned on canceling my participation in that conference but pushed through those feelings to get myself there. Then the opportunity to speak was offered and I said yes; I chose yes to move forward and do this even though it felt very uncomfortable. I made a commitment to share what I have learned about grief and loss and to form and find a community that could share this universal emotion. I moved from my inward darkness outward into compassion. I started the climb out of the deep well I was in. You must watch for these opportunities to say yes. The gifts of grief often open up your heart in a new way.

I spend more time these days focusing on what is growing and what has grown out of my grief and loss. It is a choice to take this viewpoint and still process each of the bouts of sadness as they come. Because I have loved, I grieve. There are times when I feel two polar opposite emotions like sadness and joy at the same time as I'm processing some memories. One of the people I interviewed for this book, Tom, said that he was struck the first time he realized he could be feeling two opposite emotions at the same time. It is a strange thing to experience, but one it's important to realize is totally normal.

Hope Comes

At some point, hope becomes a choice. I say it in this way because when you are buried in sadness day after day after day, hope may not feel like anything you can reach for, but you can. The first step is to begin paying attention to what emotions you find yourself experiencing on a consistent basis. There are ways, such as writing in some form, to track what is happening in your inner landscape. Begin by recording a word or finding an image that describes how you feel. Many times just recognizing emotions and naming them and giving them image or form is a way of starting to process them. Start tracking and writing down one thing that happened that moved you forward in the day.

Finding balance in your days is a first step to movement

toward hope. By tracking your emotions, whether you have chosen to write in a journal each day or just write a word that describes how you feel, you are registering this and doing an activity that is moving you forward. By naming something, even if it is that you drank water to keep your body hydrated, or you ate something nourishing, or you walked outside—these are all things that can help you see you are still creating movement in some way.

There may come a day, as it did for me after months and months of going back into despondent, sad days, when you just decide, "I don't want to feel like this today." I remember the day this happened to me clearly. I was sitting on my couch back in one of my moods in which I did not want to do anything. I lived right by the river and even putting on my tennis shoes to go for a walk didn't sound appealing. I felt like I had developed some kind of anxiety that made it impossible to make a decision. I was tired of that too, as it was often this low-level anxiety that would take me right into non-action and deciding not to do anything or go anywhere. This just compounded my mood and made me sadder. On some logical, conscious level I knew I was just making things worse, but I felt that I could not make the choice to do anything.

So, I was sitting on my couch, feeling that kind of low-level anxiety that had kept me from taking any action, which led to that familiar sadness and lethargy. I turned my head to the right, as if that was some action in itself, and heard somewhere in myself, "I don't want to feel this way today." Then that part of myself rose up again and this time said, "I choose joy."

Things Begin to Turn Around

When I heard myself say, "I choose joy," I got up off the couch and decided to go out and put gas in my car. Once I was in that direction, I decided to continue that familiar route, which usually included a trip to Whole Foods. I bought a couple of things and went back home. It may seem like such a simple thing but pay attention to the small actions you take and how you feel about taking them. It may be a baby step but acknowledge in yourself that you took one small step. These small steps are what begin to pave the way for greater action.

Having a choice about how you feel is an important aspect to understand. When you are so locked in emotions that consume you during the day and haunt you during the night, it feels as though you have no choice. Negative emotions have effects on physiology that also make it harder to turn the tide—but you can! Learning about the physiological effects of stress you experience during loss can be helpful so that you understand there are things happening that are flowing directly from the emotions you are feeling. It is in that same understanding that you can learn how renewing emotions change your physiology in a positive direction. You have a great capacity to affect what is happening to you, even though in the deepest darkness you may not feel like you do. Learning how to do breathing practices can be very helpful. It is the most basic thing we do, and watching your own breath rise and fall can become a meditative practice in itself.

Connecting to your heart, even though it may feel broken, is another step that can help. Becoming aware and working with your senses adds to your connection to the world around you. It also helps you realize you are not alone—you are in charge of your own will and you have the power to choose.

Chapter 4

FGround37

––––––– · ✦ · –––––––

When grief enters your life it can be completely disorienting. Grief is not an emotion or an experience that is expressed until a devastating loss occurs. I have wondered how, as a culture, we might change or at least make the experience and/or conversation of grief more accessible. I recently hosted a Death Café, which is part of my own mission to make the conversation about death more comfortable and acceptable. Maybe if we talk about it more death will be known as a part of life and not feared as much. Death Cafés have now been offered in 59 countries. They are group-directed discussions of death with no agenda, objectives, or themes. The conversation is generated by the people who attend.

My First Experience

I remember two overriding emotional memories after my

little brother Martin died in 1993: unbearable pain and unconditional love. My brother had three women who tended to him in his short 2½-month attempt to cure his cancer. My mother, his girlfriend, and I were always there, always present and on autopilot from the time we parked in the parking lot to his room at Stanford Hospital cancer ward—FGround37. He was never alone, and neither were we. The nurses knew us as fellow residents in his room and made sure whoever spent the night was comfortable and that we always had what we needed.

I remember thinking how glad I was that I was living so close to him. I had been accepted at U.C. Davis and U.C. Berkeley and had almost decided to stay in Sacramento with the life I had built and go to U.C. Davis. But I decided to have a whole new adventure and go to Berkeley and, for so many reasons, I'm glad I did. The best (or worst) of those reasons was that I was close enough to drive down every day after school to be with my brother Martin as he underwent treatment.

My Brother Had Become My Best Friend

I come from a family of four siblings, myself and three brothers. My youngest brother and I grew quite close over the years before his death. He came to live with me the summer between his first and second year of college. We seemed to be asking the same questions about life and shared openly and easily with each other. We challenged our upbringing in the church, which was a healthy discussion to finding our own spiritual truth. Our philosophical conversations would always lead to laughter and just having fun. I missed him terribly when he left for New York for the next three years.

After completing his undergraduate work, he attended Santa Clara Law School in California. I was so happy he made this choice because I was living in Sacramento and we saw each other often. I had finally gotten serious about school and completed all of my lower division work at community college in Sacramento. I applied and got in to U.C. Berkeley, and chose to go there instead of U.C. Davis to be closer to my brother. We supported each other through tough times and had so much laughter together. He was a source of strength in my life.

When he got so sick and realized he didn't just have the flu, he was admitted to Santa Clara County Hospital but was quickly moved to Stanford Medical Center, which had the best care available and more options for experimental drug therapies for leukemia.

I missed my finals and remember how different my teachers were in being supportive, or not supportive, of this choice I made to be with my brother. The stress I was under as a pre-med student majoring in Molecular and Cell Biology at one of the most competitive schools in the world was eclipsed by my love for my brother. The only choice I felt in my heart was to be with him. Love was my

41

choice. The years of intensity I had spent getting into Berkeley as an older undergraduate student were put into perspective by this one emotion that I still to this day experience and explore and share with great reverence and sacredness. It was the one force in my life that would be the strand that wove through the next twenty-five years of many more losses. Unconditional love, love in the face of loss, self-compassionate love to keep moving forward.

Trying to Cope

After my little brother died, I felt like my world had collapsed and become small, like the only thing left in my life was pain. I couldn't understand why this feeling wouldn't budge. I lived alone in California and after the services were done and everyone went on with their lives I found I could not. I visited Sacramento often, a place I had called home for ten years before moving to San Francisco. I remember visiting my good friend Sheryl, who had just had her second child. There was something healing in that—to recognize that just as life ends, life begins. It felt good to be around birth after spending the last couple months around death.

I wasn't able to handle the thought of rigorous study and competition, so I took a semester off from school. I spent a month on the east coast. Mom and Dad had moved to Virginia and both had jobs in Washington D.C., and most of my extended family lived in the surrounding area. It was helpful to be away for a while and I felt fortunate to be able to just take a leave from my part-time jobs and school.

When I returned home to San Francisco, I worked extra time to keep myself occupied until I could start school again. I was happy to have a Biochemistry class for 6 weeks in the summer. It was all-consuming and I met a new friend I studied with and felt a shared camaraderie in preparing to go to med school.

As life returned to "normal," to all outsiders it may have appeared that I had moved back into my life successfully. On the inside though, I was a mess. I found that anger had become a constant companion. I was mad at my brother for leaving me. In grief there is no logic to what you feel at times, but that is what I felt a lot of the time. I would have thoughts like, *That is not what we agreed to*, or, *We had so much left to do together*. School became exceedingly difficult and at times when I was faced with tests I would fall apart and not be able to perform.

I went to the university health clinic and had weekly appointments with a therapist for the rest of the semester. Each week I saved up my tears and looked forward to having a place to go and just cry. Many well-meaning people said things that didn't help at all. I relied on my weekly sanity hour. Sanity at that time was being able to cry and be really real about how I felt. I was given steps to take and activities to do in order to keep moving forward in my journey of grief.

I also remember that two distinct things happened—I stopped saying I love you, and I stopped taking pictures. I felt as though "I love you" had been thrown around in ways that were half-meant, almost like a habit that people really didn't think about. I also found when I did attend church, which was rare, I felt the same thing—words were just being said without entering into the fullness of what the contents held. In my own experience I wanted prayers to be full of meaning, building a connection to spiritual beings that I was in relationship with, if I was going to say them.

I had anger but not anger at God, as I knew some people in grief had. My relationship with God was intact, I think in part due to some of the reading I had been doing in prior years about soul journeys, soul families, past lives, and other topics of the day in New Age reading. I had no evidence but the expansion of thinking beyond what I had grown up with allowed me to keep my understanding of God alive while I explored other possibilities. It did not, however, provide any comfort at the time for the purely human emotions of deep loss that I was feeling. I came to realize over time that this in fact was the journey, the great work, of being in human bodies doing this work. Purifying emotions, rising out of the ashes like the Phoenix, finding the seed of what was being born in my life out of the ashes. Most days in that first year I didn't feel I was up to the task, nor did I see it with any clarity.

I met my husband-to-be a few months after Martin died in 1993. When we parted thirteen years later, I found myself in some kind of ricochet effect of grief, like I hadn't really processed it. In the face of moving through a very painful parting with my husband, what was left undone with my brother came to the surface.

I share this with you to caution you that grief can be underlying and seemingly invisible in your life if you've buried it or pushed it aside in any way. When I look at how I lived life, it was in some level of denial. At the time I met my husband I needed a gentle soul to comfort me in my immense pain. I shifted all the responsibility of dealing with my pain off myself to a place where I just didn't look at it. In all respects I was happy, but in retrospect I had not fully dealt with and accepted this loss, and what remained was eroding what was possible in our relationship.

My Soul Needed Solace

Years later and after several more experiences of grief with losing friends, my soul was questioning everything. I realized that this grief thing had way more to do with some larger part of my Being that was having an experience. It seemed I didn't have any contact with that part of myself. On the surface I lived a life of happy denial. I was very successful in school, completing my bachelor's and then master's degree and starting my own business in the fitness and wellness industry. I decided not to go to medical school when I realized how much I loved working in fitness and wellness. It was a wise decision and I am still glad I listened to that inner part of myself. I married at age 38, bought a new house, went on beach vacations every year. The part of me who needed spiritual answers to my sadness that lay underneath the veneer of pool parties, traveling, and destination running vacations with friends finally asserted itself.

In 2002 I began to delve into deep spiritual teachings and learn about parts of myself that I had hidden in my psyche because they were too painful. As I kept probing and turning over stones in my life (leaving no stone unturned) to see what was hidden underneath, I became demanding of my husband to do the same, questioning him relentlessly about his own life and our relationship that began to feel more superficial as the years went by. Eventually the space created between the two of us grew too big, and led to us releasing each other. I love him for how he shielded me from the pain in that time of my life, but I felt like I had taken on a quest that I could not turn away from and it had created a deep divide between us. I had done important soul work with him and released him into his life, and thereafter he returned to someone he had been in a relationship with before we met and they are now happily married.

What drove this insatiable desire to understand the world of Spirit came from a profound experience I had with my little brother Martin shortly after he died in 1993. While my religious upbringing didn't provide for understanding, I always had the sense that the "other" world was not that far away and that the connection was real between myself and the world of Spirit and those who have departed.

My brother provided me with clear evidence of communication between this world and the next after he died. I had returned to school and always started my day at a coffee shop near the Berkeley BART station. While sitting in there one morning thinking of my day ahead, an arising of what seemed like a clear perception of my brother appeared in the upper right area of the coffee shop. I could not see him but I had such a clear knowing that it was him, and I silently asked, "Martin???" He proceeded to show me that he was "there" and doing his work of helping other patients who were crossing the threshold, dying, from diseases as he had. The name of the person he provided was someone I could validate. She had passed on within the last 12 hours. This brought such comfort and validation to something I had believed for many years—that we do move on to a different space in a different form, that there is a connection to our loved ones that remains.

While parts of my Catholic faith I had been raised with remained sacred to me at that time in my life, I felt a void in its support. It did not make sense to me that there were intermediaries to go through to enter into the spiritual realms. It also did not make sense to me that crosses held the suffering Jesus, that crucifixion was the most prominent symbol upon entering a church or cathedral when the greatest message of this spiritual act was

47

resurrection! Why did we not have constant conversation about what this means? Why did we not apply reverent striving to find resurrection in our own life and activities? I found esoteric schooling that began to fill the void. I entered and completed a four-year program in a Twelve Gate Egyptian Mystery School, studying esoteric philosophy and hermetic science. I also began a seven-year apprenticeship in Shamanism. I was trained in Reiki and Pranic healing. I wanted to understand much more about that experience with my little brother Martin when he communicated with me from beyond the physical world.

The question that usually flares in the deep emotion of grief is, "What is my life for now?" It is important to see that the questions you are asking are about you, about your experience still living, now without the other who defined a part of your existence. In the swirl of the contracted life I felt I was living, the most helpful teachings were about Soul contracts and our experiences with others in our life as a means of growth and learning through love and pain. I found the work of Anthroposophy and it provided a picture so large, a cosmos filled with spiritual beings, a history of spiritual evolution of man. Anthroposophy roughly translates to "the wisdom of being human" and provides a path of knowledge to guide the spiritual in us human beings to the spiritual in the universe. It offers a body of knowledge, methods, and practices that embodies the wisdom of the great traditions and offers the modern spiritual seeker a path of understanding. I finally felt rooted in something that made my small contracted world begin to expand. I continue to study and strive to tend to my inner work as a spiritual being. When emotional experiences are so dense it is helpful to have a bigger picture that helps me see the activity of my body, soul, and spirit—it lightens the denseness of a purely physical experience.

I realized that all those years ago I had closed off the part of myself that had been having direct experiences in the spiritual world, and now I was reawakening it. When my little brother was in treatment for his cancer I had several experiences with the spiritual realm, but I had no context for understanding them at the time. I drove every day from San Francisco to Palo Alto to Stanford Medical Hospital along the Highway 280 corridor. I had the habit of staying in silence for the whole 45 minute drive and often I perceived a rising, some sort of calling out from the groves of trees that lined the freeway on the right. I had no vocabulary or understanding of what was happening; I just knew it was and I trusted it. I was fully conscious and had no reason to think I was off my rocker!

In these perceptions I saw/knew/heard that my brother would die and was somehow comforted in this knowing that seemed to be arising out of the trees. Like there was some larger wisdom at play that I could not reach in my thinking mind, but in my silent heart connection while traveling to be with my brother, mother, and Martin's girlfriend, I could accept this truth. Somehow it helped to know there was something larger at play than my thinking mind could understand.

Grief as a Practice

To become better at grief you must recognize and live fully in the rhythms of death and rebirth. Mourning a loss and adjusting to life is part of the process after a loss. The ability to move fully into this loss and recognize the rebirth happening at the same time is another level of understanding. What I mean by this is that oftentimes there is something growing out of the experience and you may not see it until later. It's like a tapestry is being woven when you look back at a particular point in your life. Trust that you are weaving into the tapestry now if you are in the depths of your grieving. It is the richness of colors both dark and light woven into a life that creates beauty.

As the part of you that had a connection to the one you loved continues to die, there is an opportunity to see through your heart that the connection is never lost. One way in which you can become more agile with the heaviness of loss is to actively cultivate this connection in a new way. Staying connected to your loved one is possible, but it is out of a greater part of yourself, a part of yourself that has grown out of your soul connection with another. My little brother Martin gave me a gift in showing me that communication is real; it is palpable. I believe that out of my experience, Martin was showing me that we all can stay more connected to the spiritual world.

If you are not already, choose some inspirational or devotional readings to read to your lost loved one. When saying prayers, know that they are received. I have had intuitive experiences with all of my other family members who have died. I cherish this level of experience; it helps me to see that there is a part of us that continues.

Chapter 5

Surrender

———— · ✷ · ————

It is never too early to start working with your grief. In fact, recognizing it along the way for me as my big brother was going through his process with chemo and radiation treatments helped me tremendously. I needed to talk about what was happening but my family did not. I think my brother felt if he talked about dying he would be admitting defeat. My sadness was deep and I needed to be able to express it.

Know that sadness, confusion, and helplessness are all emotions that are a normal part of grief, and expressing them is important to your journey. Finding places and ways to do that will help keep you from getting buried too deeply in your grief.

Finding Helpful Hearts

Pay attention and spend time with those people in your life who can listen openly and allow you to express your feelings. Many people are so uncomfortable with the range of emotions that grief can bring and may say things that are very unhelpful. They say these things trying to be helpful, but they end up hurtful because the other person is unable to be with the depth of emotion you are feeling. I remember how many people said to me, "He's in a better place," when my little brother died at the age of 28. I had to hide my inner rage and desire to lash out at this comment. It was the last thing I wanted to hear. I wanted him *here* with *me*, not somewhere else. I realized that this was coming from spiritual beliefs that held the understanding that he was in heaven; he was with God. But I just wanted to express my feelings about how awful it was that he was not here with me anymore.

Pay attention and recognize those individuals in your life who have the ability to just listen and allow you to express whatever you need to. You may find these people by reaching out in your community. It can be helpful to meet others in a group setting with a shared set of circumstances. Shared experiences and stories help you recognize that you are not alone. While your experience is uniquely yours, finding connection may bring comfort in a shared understanding of the experience. This may be particularly helpful for those who have experienced loss through violent death or suicide of a loved one. If what you need is an objective ear and heart, a spiritual advisor or family therapist may provide more comfort.

Surrender

You may not recognize yourself in the depth of emotions that you express while lost in the river of grief. I remember coming home from a couple of social gatherings and falling onto the floor in sobs as soon as I got through the door. It felt so over the top, so dramatic, and yet that was me having that experience. It was cleansing and moved the buildup of emotion I had been holding back in the social situation I was in. That's an example of something I will repeat throughout this book—the only way out is in…and then through.

While I am not saying to dwell in your negative emotions, you do want to acknowledge them and take some kind of action in feeling what you are feeling, so you can move through it. It is often the fear that you will never get out of the overwhelming sadness that keeps you from surrendering to it. At times the right action may be to just BE in it. Being consumed by sadness is not comfortable, and yet, the more you try to push it away the worse it gets. There is an interesting effect that occurs by consciously allowing yourself to step into the feeling and just be there. This is a counter-intuitive move, isn't it? When I look at all the ways there are in our society to *not* feel, it takes something to surrender. Expanding fully into yourself and your experience when your experience is completely dark takes courage, but what is gained out of doing that is great wisdom.

I've always loved the works of David Whyte and his soulful words in poetry. Here is an excerpt from one of his poems, "The Well of Grief," which paints a beautiful picture of the invitation of grief: "Those who will not slip beneath the still surface on the well of grief, turning down through its black water to a place you cannot breathe, will never know the source from which we drink..." There is a depth of beauty for those who surrender to this journey.

So, as a practice, as a way to work with your grief, step into it...surrender. While you are in this place, this state of what likely feels like deep darkness, find some way to express what it is you are experiencing. A journal is a good place to start and in later chapters I will outline a process that is more structured with imagery. For now, though, consider keeping a journal of this sacred experience. This is an experience of death and rebirth, and great possibility awaits you if you let yourself enter into this work willingly. A part of you is dying and a part of you is being birthed; this is a Soul experience.

When you willingly surrender and enter into the darkness you are feeling, you can ask questions of the darkness, ask your Soul that is having this experience, and wait for what comes up as an answer. Here are some questions you may want to pose to yourself:

- What is here in this darkness?

- If my body is in my soul, what does my soul know here in this darkness?

- What is true and what would be healing here?

Action and Healing

Taking action in the face of daunting sadness is not a skill that is taught, but I've learned from my years spent as a spiritual healer that the body and psyche store much of what we do not process through our day-to-day experience of trauma, loss, and grief. I believe that depression and anxiety can result out of this inability to enter into the ongoing death and rebirth that is happening in your own life on a daily basis. Being faced with a great loss in your life is often the spiritual impulse to call you to this work.

Everyday needs for self-care need to be considered as well. Making the smallest decisions may seem difficult for a long time. If this is true for you too, there are a couple of things you can do to help in this very practical need: Ask others to provide extra communication and reminders of activities and commitments. Make your needs known if having the option to back out at the last minute is needed. I had to buy a day-at-a-glance calendar so that I could see things on paper.

Many well-meaning people say that grief just takes time. What I've found to be true is that time takes on a different quality. It can be difficult to track time when you are showing up in your life and trying to get back to a normal routine and are still aware that you are processing deep emotional upheaval. While it is true that over time you may start functioning better, this will only happen if you are taking actions to move forward in your thoughts and feelings.

Grief Can Be Cumulative

I had to take many steps to remain stable in all the emotions I was experiencing after my big brother Michael passed away recently. I found myself reliving the whole past twenty-five years of sadness and loss. My family of six is now just two of us. While I made the decision to not have children and I've never regretted it, the aloneness that I felt was daunting. It felt like a bookend from the time my little brother died to when my big brother died. After the funeral ended and my younger brother and his wife went home to Ohio, we formed a deeper relationship and continue to FaceTime with each other weekly. It is a sweet friendship that continues to grow and we get to talk about some of the memories of our life and family together.

There was a deeper need that arose from the sadness this time and it felt much more existential and needy in me. This time it was about my own destiny, the fulfillment of my life. Each time a loss occurs, the question of "Who am I?" comes up. Having barely processed the loss of my dad and the feeling of being rootless, the loss of my big brother compounded the attempt to identify myself. With each loss it is necessary to see the beauty of the work that was done in relationship with that person, and then to take in the gifts and fullness of whatever that life brought and begin the work of identifying and growing into the person you are now without the other.

Spiritual Teachings

Many of the teachings I've learned during my quest to make sense of life and death have helped me keep moving through grief each time I've been in it. I've learned from many cultural practices and always held to my Christian understanding and the mysteries of Christ. I see the death and resurrection of Jesus Christ as a universal event that is set against the backdrop of all prior spiritual evolution of humans, and those who have come before and moved human evolution forward through their deeds and teachings. My understanding is inclusive of all that came before as an additive to what humanity is currently moving through as a spiritual impulse.

My view is that we co-create with Divine Beings the life we come to on Earth. When we leave, we take with us what we have purified and learned and do work of some kind in the spiritual realm. Then we determine the next life and bring with us what we need and plan particular tasks and learning. You do not need to believe as I do on these matters, but I think it was important for me to share my views as they relate to this topic of birth and death.

In later years during my shamanic apprenticeship, I learned the terminology "ordinary consciousness" and "non-ordinary consciousness" to describe the space of here and there. These terms are used to speak of the realm of Spirit and the realm of matter. For instance, when you walk out into a wooded area with birds chirping and sun glistening down through the trees, in ordinary consciousness you are experiencing it through your senses. In non-ordinary consciousness, you have deliberately sought a connection with the spiritual world and you're experiencing some sense of the Spirit of the oak tree, or the message of winged ones (known as the messengers between the worlds). In most traditions there are levels of worlds (upper world, middle world, and lower world) in which you find different spiritual beings. In Celtic traditions there is a hidden world behind the realm of our five-sense experience, spoken of as slipping into the mists. In shamanic cultures, rattles or drums are used to journey into these realms to receive information and messages. Meditative practices also produce this connection with the spiritual realm. You can study and meditate on the growth of a rose, for instance, forwards and back, forwards and back, death and rebirth, and begin to connect to the spirit behind the rose. Many people who spend a great deal of time in nature report a deeper sense of connection with the world. In my understanding there are beings behind all things and I walk in reverence at times in recognition.

Meditation and mindfulness are now part of worksite wellness programs and provide the training of inner silence. There is great interest in spiritual practice and energy healing and greater attendance in churches. These things are, I believe, a reflection of the deep questioning in people's hearts to understand a greater connection to higher self, to Soul, to Spirit.

My studies in Anthroposophy (the wisdom of being human) provided, and continue to provide, the most full and open invitation to this understanding. I learned of a cosmology of the planets and epochs of time full of spiritual beings that are a part of my evolution as a human. The more I learned of this expansive nature of being human, the more grounded I felt and the more I was able to find meaning in my struggles and suffering. Anthroposophy was brought to humanity through Rudolf Steiner, Austrian-born philosopher (1861-1925) and modern day initiate (a person born with extraordinary capacities). He contributed more than 6000 recorded public lectures and 40 books. The volumes and volumes of lectures and studies in Anthroposophy filled hours and hours of my time and I learned of teachings about the nine realms of Angelic hierarchies and how we are the tenth, the Beings of Love and Freedom.

Our modern day task individually and collectively is to build morality out of freedom. As I continued to reflect on what all of the experiences of grief were offering in my life, I felt that they had something to do with this. I kept coming back to the invitation to expand my heart, to love in a bigger way, to find beauty even in the deepest pain. Can I love enough to let go of all want and need in myself, to just hold another in their process? I could not when my little brother Martin died, but when my big brother Michael was facing death I kept finding the pain balanced by such love! I visited as often as I could to be with him and his family and felt I was learning how to love better and more unconditionally with each visit. Knowing that there is some deeper understanding and some larger picture in these events helped me to keep moving into a bigger, more expansive love, and it helped with the suffering. I have recognized that this kind of love is a rare occurrence and I consider it is a gift out of grief to have found this experience of unconditional love.

The gift of grief for some can be this opening to a deeper aspect of Soul and Spirit. Rudolf Steiner often spoke of wisdom as crystallized pain. I remember when I first read that it reminded me of something my mom always used to tell me. At twenty when I moved from the state of Washington to California, I was bound and determined to make a new life for myself. I loved my family dearly but something inside me wanted a kind of independence and I didn't feel like I could get it staying near the family home. I was so homesick for the first two years and on occasion

I would start crying on the phone when I was talking to Mom. She was never a coddler (and that's probably where I got my independence!) and so she would tell me, "You'll be just fine—this is building character."

Growing Through Grief

Chapter 6

Taking Care of Self

———— · ✴ · ————

I have come to understand the experiences I've had in my life through various teachings of life, death, and rebirth, and my relationship with the spiritual world. These may not be yours and that is okay. Grief is a time that can challenge but also expand your beliefs. Connections to our loved ones still exist, just in a different form. The main point here is that you are still HERE and they are there, however and wherever that is for you. Now is the time for you to take charge of yourself here, creating steps to understand who you are now. There is a purpose for your life, and there are lessons at a soul level available for you to learn. To orient to this newness is the job at hand. Taking care of your body may seem inconsequential as you try to process loss, but taking steps in your own care can help you on the road to moving through grief.

Starting Here

My friend Jenna shared with me that in the days right after her boyfriend's death, she had the weird sensation that she needed to remind herself to breathe. Everything that had been automatic or voluntary seemed to require thought. For two and a half months she had spent all her time by his side, tending and caring for him and supporting him. The shock of him dying left such a large hole that it was difficult to fill with anything. Most things felt so meaningless.

The disorientation that comes with grief can be unsettling. As my friend shared, even breathing can feel foreign! A couple of tools can help with this. Paying attention to your body's needs is a first step in beginning the reorientation to your life. It's important in the initial days after a loss to eat, drink, move, and sleep as best you can. Trust that biology will drive this, as most people including myself cannot eat or sleep much the first couple days. The adrenaline pumping through your body overrides hunger at first. I'm always amazed at how generous people are in coming to the aid of another. When my mother died, my two brothers, their families, and my dad were cared for with food and drink for nearly a week. It's always something I remember and I watch for the opportunity to pay it forward. Sleeping can be difficult so let yourself rest and sleep during the day if you can.

What is the Next Best Thing You Can Do?

When you feel unable to get out of a state of disorientation or overwhelm, ask yourself, "What can I do right now?" Or another version of this is, "What is the next best thing I can do?" Pause and wait to see what bubbles up as an answer. I learned this from my yoga teacher as a way to be present with my body's needs throughout the day. It is a type of mindfulness practice but more importantly, during grief, it can help you form some kind of action during times when you may not feel like pulling the covers back from sleep. It is also a way to help you recognize that your body has an inner wisdom and to start connecting more deeply to it. In times of crisis you may find a strength you did not know you had. Trust that you have the answers within.

This is a good time to practice a meditation/visualization called the body scan. The typical body scan meditation takes you through each part of your body in succession. I add an additional step of bringing love to each of those parts. I find this so helpful at night when I'm awakened and can't get back to sleep. Here is how to do this:

1. Bring your attention to the top of your head.

2. Say to yourself, "I love myself for…"

3. State something at each part of your body. For example, at my head I say "my intellect" or "my ability to think clearly." At my thighs I might say

something like "my thighs that help move me forward through the day." Don't get stuck on this part of finding words—just move down through your body, naming each part or focusing on each part.

4. If you fall asleep while focusing on your throat—great! If you wake up again, pick up the meditation right where you left off and start at your shoulders.

Here's another helpful activity to stay connected to your body that can bring comfort quickly: Find something soft to hold on to and keep bringing softness to your skin by wrapping yourself in it or caressing your face. In some of my discussions with people, someone shared that she also used this as a way to calm her nervous system and anxiety when she was driving. All of your senses may be extra sensitive and open to input that you find calming. Pay attention to what helps.

I recall having an experience that seemed extra sensitive with my vision. I was getting out of the car to go in to a friend's house and noticed the flowers along the sidewalk border and front porch were very vivid. I blinked my eyes, thinking I couldn't be seeing what I was seeing. They seemed to have about five times the color depth than usual. When I left my friend's house, I noticed that this sensory expansion was gone—the flowers looked how they normally did to my vision. My initial experience felt like a gift to me, like something of the spiritual world was meeting me.

While grieving is a time when you may not feel like even inhabiting your body, it is also a time when you can expand self-compassion and recognize that your body is your vehicle. Think of how diamonds are formed in intense heat and pressure. Many form somewhere between 87 and 118 miles underground in the Earth's mantle. Carbon-containing minerals provide the raw materials for this formation. You, too, are undergoing intense pressure and "fire." What if what is happening in your body, emotions, and thoughts is purifying something, changing you, challenging you and all of your beliefs? It is up to you whether you choose to look at what is happening over time as a lessening of yourself, or a growing into something new with a particular beauty.

Emotions of Grief

Emotions have a powerful effect on your physiology. In times of grief, while you may not want to experience what you are feeling, the more you can do to acknowledge and move what you are feeling, or at least just move your body, the less inclined you will be to get stuck in other addictive habits that are detrimental to you long-term.

As a trainer and coach, I have led many people through the practices from the Institute of HeartMath®. The initial step in all of these techniques is to bring your attention and awareness to your heart. Additional steps include choosing and activating an emotion that is renewing. More than any other thing you do, staying connected to your heart is healing. While it may be difficult to choose any other state of being on some days, at least connect to your heart and pay attention to your breathing. Imagining that your breath is moving through your heart settles your nervous system to some extent. On the emotional level, your heart has loved and your heart may feel shattered or like it has a hole in it. Learning to connect to your heart daily, no matter what you are feeling, is a practice, a discipline that may bring unexpected gifts. There is a beauty in being human and having the capacity for this range of emotions. Being able to experience love to the degree that you did reflects in the pain that you may be feeling.

I spoke earlier about choosing joy. I recall another day when this simple declaration brought movement forward in me. I was driving around doing errands, stuck in the heaviness of my deeply somber mood. I could feel the draw to buy a bottle of wine and numb out for the rest of the day. Instead I actively decided to choose joy. Now, I didn't expect that I would have a state of joy descend upon me that would make me start singing a happy song. I couldn't even reach for a state that felt close to that mentally or emotionally. What I did notice, though, was that I was able to connect with people in the store instead of staying in my sullen mood. I felt my heart opening as I bantered back and forth with the grocery store clerk and I noticed it was my simple act of choosing that allowed me to extend myself out of my inner world of sadness. I had been training myself for so long with the HeartMath® techniques that my mind knew this tool of choosing, but in my deep sadness the overwhelming emotions made it difficult to see I had made a habit of being sad and I just needed to focus my habits back in the other direction!

If you would like to learn more about HeartMath® and participate in guided meditations, there is a beautiful project called the Global Coherence Initiative. You may find it beneficial to participate in the free offering. On the site https://www.HeartMath®.org/gci/ you can follow a guided script in the Global Care Room and also see that you are connecting to other hearts around the world.

Learning to Choose

Learning to refocus on yourself after caring for someone else for a lengthy period of time can be daunting. If loss has occurred as a result of caring for another, you may feel relieved at first, but the feelings of deep loss will quickly follow. It helps to have or make a goal for yourself that then requires steps forward to meet that goal. Recognizing that finishing school was an immediate need helped my friend Jenna on her grief journey to move back into her life. The hole that had been created by months of spending time by her boyfriend's side felt like it couldn't be filled, but school was there when she was ready to get back to it. Day by day, having details to attend to and work to do, she was able to start focusing more on her own life.

Whether you are choosing to just drink a glass of water, or move off the couch to put gas in the car, or go back to school or work—recognize that you are in charge of choosing. Each time you make a small choice and take action, you are strengthening yourself. While the emotions of grief and loss may feel overwhelmingly dense and intense, recognize that here too you have choice. I remember watching the movie *Dangerous Lives*, a movie about a teacher at an inner city school. The teacher's class was filled with kids who often chose to join gangs, sell drugs, or just not show up for school. After becoming fed up with their complaining about having to be in school, she very passionately pointed out that each day they made a choice. They could stay out on the street and invite trouble, or they could show up to school, get an education, and make their lives better. She had them see that there is always a choice, even if you may not like the choice. Being able to choose is a human birthright and one that sets us apart from the animal and plant world.

Here is one more tool that you can use to help build the muscle of choosing. Every day, either when you get up or when you go to bed (or both!), ask yourself, "What beauty have I seen/experienced today?" If you cannot find anything—look outside and notice a tree, a bush, or a flower, and acknowledge the beauty of life you see.

Chapter 7

Gaining a New Perspective
—— · ✦ · ——

By now you might be hearing an underlying tone to my message—that you have all you need within you to get through the struggle and suffering you may be feeling. If your pain has moved to a deep suffering sense of aloneness, from a spiritual perspective you may have entered into a "Dark Night of the Soul." This is a sacred experience in which you may feel completely alone and the work in this aloneness is to find yourself, to move yourself through, to discover what is on the other side of pain. Our culture has little to offer in support of this passage from a spiritual perspective. The inclination on a personal level is to check out with some kind of addictive behavior. The practice in our medical community is to provide pharmaceutical soothing.

This is one of the greatest times of growth and courage and potential, and there is little in our experience that can teach us how to move through it. Remain open in your experience—this is also a time when you may find resources that shift the path of your life.

Feeling Anchorless

I once asked a counselor what made the difference in people who experience feelings of suicide but don't act on it and those who do. She responded that those who have activities and habits that allow for continuous expression of what they are feeling maintain an ability to keep moving through. Depending on the circumstances and situation, some who are suffering in grief may go to an extreme sense that life is not worth living anymore; without this other person there is no purpose. I implore you to recognize that your feelings of devastation are natural and normal. *Please*, if you are experiencing thoughts of suicide, here are some resources that can provide you with immediate assistance: the national Suicide Prevention Lifeline (1-800-273-8255) and the Crisis Text Hotline (text to 741741 in the U.S.) The text hotline is active in Canada as well through Ontario's Online and Text Crisis and Distress Service from 2pm-2am.

I have wondered at times how I got through the excruciatingly painful days I lived through these last ten years. As a spiritual healer I could not understand why I was suffering so—was I not somewhat immune because of the preparation and practice that I had? The answer to that is a resounding no! It does mean, however, that I had a very strong context of understanding that I could continually move into, which provided an anchor for me. When I began to view the pain, the suffering, and depression as the vehicle to my own growth, I began to experience my days differently.

Those who know that well of sadness, grief, and depression describe it in different ways. For me it often felt like quicksand and on some days I wanted to surrender to the pull of the quicksand and couldn't feel in me a desire to do anything but surrender to death.

My own surrender to death! When that thought occurred to me out of the feeling that I really didn't care if I lived or died, I heard the call to suicide. I had been here before, the first time when I was fifteen years old. There was no sense of acting on it but the consideration of it was heavy in me. So, knowing that I would not act on it, I kept wallowing around in the muck. It's kind of a surrender in itself, a "well, since I'm here I might as well explore what's here" kind of feeling.

In that exploration and wallowing in the depths I recognized that SOMETHING in me needed to die, but not all of me did.

This was a turning point! It felt like succumbing to the lure of death, not a choice. But the choice came when I could clearly see this reality and distinction that *part* of me was ready to die—not all of me. The heaviness and darkness and loneliness of grief are so impactful that death feels welcoming. And it is a death of sorts, but not of the body; rather, it's a death of some subtle part of your being (different traditions have descriptions of these "invisible" parts of our being and I leave it to you, the reader, to take your own perspective here). I believe our lack of ritual, of training, of ignorance to the exploration of the shadow (as Carl Jung called it) has placed us in a crisis of consciousness that needs work and healing! This is where myth and story as in the work of Joseph Campbell is meaningful. It can also be helpful to relate your own experience through the myth framework.

There is a story of the Sumerian Goddess Inanna, from ancient Mesopotamian myths, who willingly enters a path of initiation and descends to the underworld, submitting to experiences to understand her dark side. In the act of acceptance we all open the doorway to receiving as we traverse what is there to understand in this universal experience of grief. I think that was part of the turning point for me, when I just decided that the depression and darkness I was experiencing held something for me to learn. When I finally sank into it with a curiosity and decision to just explore what was there in the darkness rather than try to continually push it away, it changed the experience I was having.

So back to Inanna—as the myth goes, she descends in her journey into the depths through seven gates. For three days she is hung on a hook in the underworld and stripped raw and naked. She meets her sister, Queen of the

Underworld, and then begins the ascent through seven gates of gifts and adornment as she rises. Joseph Campbell's interpretation offers the perspective that one's own strength is found through an episode of powerlessness. Through the psychological power of a descent of this nature into the unconscious and acceptance of one's own negative qualities, the result is a strengthening. This was my experience when I finally succumbed to looking around in the darkness I found myself in rather than pushing it away. The strength I found in myself was that I *could* withstand these deep emotions of loss and there was something to learn about myself in the expression of grief.

As I progressed in my exploration of the dense, muddy muck of my dark days, I saw that Death wanted to be understood. I felt confusion and fear that had no explanation in my life, despite my faith-based upbringing. I felt something was missing in my education and understanding of what it is to be a human being. This is what propelled my journey of seeking spiritual truths from many traditions. The moment you are born, death is your constant companion. Like a hidden friend by your side, death waits with a knowing sense of destiny. So death and birth are tied together and in some sense, the same thing. These thoughts pushed me to seek a much larger view of spirituality.

Cumulative Effect

Grief can come from many different events and situations in your life. The loss of a loved one, the loss of a pet, the loss of a relationship are all major events. But there are also the ongoing parts of life that often go undetected and unrecognized, like a change in parenting responsibility and the empty nest situation. Major health changes can bring deep feelings of grief as well. The inclination is to "power through" or distract or deny your feelings, but it is important to stay on top of whether you are processing and acknowledging your emotions as life's challenges face you.

At the time when my father had passed away and my brother had gotten his terminal cancer diagnosis, my own health was challenged in ways I did not acknowledge. I had been an athlete for nearly 30 years and slowly over a two-year period some injuries in my body had led to two bulging discs and a tear in my hip cartilage. I had stopped running and was struggling to keep up with yoga and Pilates. I traveled often to be with my brother as he went through treatment, and staying on top of my back pain with bodywork while maintaining my work life became extremely difficult. I was grieving the loss of my athletic self and the loss of my number one way of relieving stress. Food, caffeine, and alcohol became alternating modes of dealing with the emotions. I don't recommend it!

The Pull of Addiction

My heightened anxiety during this period led me to default back to some old patterns of using food to soothe myself. I was consciously using the tools I know for resilience and stress management, but trying to manage everything became too much. Thankfully, at that time I received an email in my inbox with the subject line, "Are You A Food Addict?" I jumped into the work of food addiction and the work of Susan Peirce Thompson and Bright Line Eating. I was so grateful that I found this work and I continue it to this day. It has helped me acknowledge many directions of addiction I had with the brain wiring I have. For example, each time I would address one thing (initially giving up flour and sugar) my coffee consumption soared. When I started weaning off of that, my wine consumption soared! So I have surrendered to being an addict and continue to stay supported in a helpful community. The most helpful communities feel loving and non-judgmental. On a group coaching call I once called the Bright Line Eating community a "container of love."

When you are experiencing deep emotions that overwhelm you, it is important to find avenues of acknowledging, expressing, and processing them. Support is important but it is also critical to pay attention to your inner work. In my own life I found it helpful to get in a rhythm of being with people and being alone and doing my own reflection. Pay attention if you are defaulting into habits that have an addictive quality. This may be a time to finally confront this addiction.

Comments from Others

If you do not have the support to talk about what you are experiencing and feeling, the pressure from others to just "get over it" can be damaging. Being in your own grief process means choosing who it is that you draw closer to you, and who you choose to distance yourself from if possible.

There may be a point at which you feel it's time to "get over it," but make sure that this comes from a place of knowing you have in place what is needed, or that you have done the work to express your feelings and pain. If you have not accomplished this it's like putting a damp blanket over a roaring fire. The fire may die back a bit but the embers will find places in your life to assert themselves. It is important to know that what you feel is part of the spectrum of emotion that makes you human. You don't want to necessarily feel it, but there it is...crap...sigh... So a better place to position yourself in is one of curiosity.

In my search for resources that could help me in my grief, I discovered the Grief Recovery Method. Founded in the mid 1980s, the method is now offered worldwide. It is a body of work that is dedicated to helping grievers take specific actions to let go of painful feelings of loss. When

I attended the Grief Recovery Method® in Reno, Nevada while I was editing this book, I found that the original experience twenty-five years earlier of losing my brother Martin still had an incompleteness to it. I was able to see that many of the experiences going forward from that time were shadowed by this incompleteness. I also believe it had something to do with the complete overwhelm and incapacitation I felt with my recent losses. Grief is cumulative.

Finding a Helpful Mindset

A helpful first step is to recognize that this (whatever *this* is) has happened. This sense of acceptance is like a doorway, an entry into a new place that provides the opportunity to see things from a new perspective. One of the things that happens in the overwhelming chaos of initial feelings of loss is a sense of aloneness. Being able to recognize that these experiences are universal can help you hold onto the knowing that others have suffered this and made it through, and that you can too. Having said that, it's also important to know that every situation is unique—don't compare.

It is often said in healing communities that a traumatic experience is Spirit's call. Some respond by becoming more devout and practicing in a particular spiritual stream, finding a new spiritual understanding, while others reject spirituality completely. Each of these is a valid response and a part of your own journey into understanding. When this is thrust upon you it does not feel like you have a choice, but as you continue to move through your process you will find you have a choice in how you are receiving and processing your experience. This often entails an expanded view beyond the physical truth of what happened.

The concept of the Dark Night of the Soul holds the promise that there is a spiritual potential that awaits all of us. The part of you that is dying must do so in order for the birth of something new to arise. Alchemy, the changing of something from one state into a higher state, requires high heat. You are in the fire when you allow yourself to just feel what you are feeling.

About the time I was writing this part of the book, Kelly Brogan, MD released an article in which she spoke of suicidality as a symptom of awakening. She is a western-trained psychiatrist and as she states, "I'm on a mission. Now, in addition to my training as a psychiatrist, I'm also board-certified in integrative and holistic medicine, helping women get healthy and happy—without drugs." She writes, "I believe suicidality to be a nearly requisite expression of urgency for change that must be met with the promise of such change being possible." One of the recommendations she has for those supporting another who may be having suicidal thoughts is to listen to them. Listen fully and completely. With this same recommendation she gives the exercise to set a timer for three minutes and hold the other person's gaze as a way to move into the heart and out of the head. This suggestion to listen fully and completely reminded me of a comment that my nephew, who drives an ambulance, said to me: "I pick up people who have attempted or were about to attempt suicide and they just need someone to hold their hand and listen." I think we are so conditioned to interrupt, to intellectualize, and to fix something that sounds like a problem that we have no idea what it is to truly listen to another human being. One of the greatest needs of a griever is to just speak, own their feelings, and be heard without interruption, without comment, without "fixing."

Even in the most horrific and dark stories of grief, newness and goodness can emerge. Joyce, who lost her twenty-year-old son to a vicious attack by two homeless men, learned that while her son lay dying on a bike trail, another homeless man came upon him and stayed with him until his last breath. As the months moved forward and Joyce's life became consumed by deepening rage and the confusion of entering into the legal system, she began to search for this homeless man who had the compassion to be with her son, to comfort him while awaiting the arrival of the police. In an interview many years after, Joyce was asked, "How did compassion become a part of your grief story?" She recounted that compassion was not necessarily present but arose as she moved in a direction of connection to this small piece of goodness that was a part of the tragic loss of her son. As this compassion grew, she pursued and secured a small space to begin serving the homeless population. Her life had been devoted to serving people as a family therapist, and she applied her skills and gifts as a therapist in service to the very population from which her son's murderers had come from. Through counsel and continued communication, the homeless man who had been by her son's side now has a small business and is a thriving member of the community.

So to recap a bit—deep dark, mucky emotions are a normal and natural response to loss. This is a part of the human experience and a universal experience. If you can take the view that you are engaged in an alchemical experience (transforming something of a lesser quality to one of higher quality) it will help you understand that to start the process of changing something, you need to be in it. Changing thoughts and feelings of loss, devastation, and utter aloneness into wisdom and understanding is your birthright and a part of the human process. Take heart and move into your heart often. Find people who can listen to you with empathy. Find community that supports you in love and acceptance. Take steps every day to surrender to this process and trust that you are gathering gifts and adornment just like Inanna did in her ascent back to life from her hook in the underworld.

Chapter 8

Finding Actions to Move Forward

——— · ✹ · ———

I will begin this chapter as I did the last—you have all that you need within you to get through the struggle and suffering you may be feeling. By example, metaphor, and myth, I have given you an invitation to understand that you are not alone, that there is a bigger context for what you are feeling, and that through struggle there is something that is dying and something that is being created in you. In my work, I find that a body, soul, and spirit approach works well to provide the widest opportunity to enter into activities that address the whole human experience.

You Just Want the Pain to Stop

Several people I spoke with about their experience with grief related the thought that they were afraid to let their tears flow because they thought they might never stop. I recall that same feeling and at times wondering where the wailing cries in me came from. I also thought at that time how normalized this wailing is in some cultures, but not in mine. Somehow that simple thought brought a freedom to my deep sobbing. Most times when I was finished I felt relief, like a holy silence for a moment.

As I have said previously—the only way out is in and through. In the big picture, whether you are speaking of this as an experience of the body, soul, or spirit, this experience is here, now, and entering into it fully is the invitation. It brings connection in ways you may not expect. Whether this is in meeting others or in having some deeper sense of the mystical nature of death and rebirth, there is something on the other side of entering the doorway of grief and finding expression of your grief in it.

There is a big distinction I would like to make in case you hear me giving you permission to enter into endless expressions of getting stuck in grief and sadness. What I mean by entering fully into the experience of grief is to enter in with an intention to learn from it and allow it to make you a fuller human being. To offer yourself fully and to turn yourself inside out to become new in some way through this experience.

Adjusting to Loss

In the bigger picture you are adjusting to a loss, a

permanent change in your life. Finding ways to help yourself express grief will help you through your life as you adjust to this loss. There are times when memories or situations will remind you of your loss and the more adept you are at processing sadness and then choosing to move forward, the more you will hold onto the good that came from loving.

Tom shared with me that the first year after the loss of his wife, he wanted to find every way he could to share the love he and his wife had experienced, the love that he still felt in his heart. He knew he could become bitter or find ways to express it. He worked with kids at Vacation Bible School, befriended homeless people, and kept feeling the sadness he felt but also finding a way to be love and to give love. Ultimately, love is what is most helpful in healing. There are so many negative emotions that can draw you into a quicksand of bitterness and sadness, but if you are active in recognizing that you are still capable of love, you can take great strides in helping yourself by having this attitude. In most of the interviews I've had with people, it was ultimately turning themselves outward in service to others that brought healing.

The biggest part of movement forward is adjusting to life without whomever, or whatever, you have lost. It is your identity that feels threatened and you may feel confusion in trying to reorient yourself to who you are in life. Eventually you may find your biggest question is, "Who am I now?" This most basic question can often get buried in the muck and mud of getting through the feelings of loss, but it is what represents the opportunity, the rebirth of yourself. I recall feeling completely anchorless and reeling in this question after my big brother died. Out of a family of six, just my younger brother and I were left and he lived across the country from me. The image that appeared for me was all of the roots of the tree being gone, having withered and died away.

What eventually happened in that image and through my own work was that I became the roots. I created ways to be closer to my family and I also created ways to serve my community more. While I was in the anchorless, rootless feeling I processed so many memories from a time when I was in my twenties and found it curious that I kept going back to that time in my memories. What I realized was that it was a time when all four of us children were going out into the world, creating our own lives full of our parents' love and finding ways to begin creating our own lives. In the metaphor of the tree, at that time I had started dropping down a thin root in my family tree and I just had to recognize that I was filling in and reaching deeper. I have spoken to many people who shared this same feeling of rootlessness in the loss of the second parent.

Practical Steps

From a practical standpoint, it is important to take care of yourself during times of grief. Your body is processing stress hormones that are triggered by all of the emotions you are experiencing. Here are some ways to help you on the physical level to process grief and keep your body healthy:

- Stop yourself and ask, "What can I do right now?" Pause and wait for an answer to come. This may seem too simplistic to bring any relief but if you build this as a habit it can become a powerful way to remain conscious of what you are experiencing. This can be helpful in stopping yourself in moments of disorientation. Build trust in the wisdom your body provides. It may be as simple as drinking some water, eating, lying down, or allowing yourself to cry.

- Get outside in the fresh air. If the sun is out close your eyes and turn your face toward the light for just a minute.

- Take a shower and as the water flows, see and feel your grief flowing—let it move. If this means sobbing, crying, or just watching it like a movie—let it move.

- Find something soft to hold onto and keep bringing softness to your skin by wrapping yourself in it or caressing your face with it. I bought a child's 12" security blanket with a lamb's head. I traveled with it and hid it in my travel carry-on bag and held on to it to relieve anxiety that I was experiencing. The lamb had significance with my mom, who was dying of a neurological degenerative disease.

- Book some kind of body work/massage. It will help you stay in touch with your own body and help move things along on a physical and an energetic level.

- Move your body in some way. Classes in yoga, tai chi, and Pilates may offer an added benefit of inner calm. Dancing is good too. As I've mentioned previously, do anything to move your body, even just swinging your arms from side to side.

- Do something with your non-dominant hand. You are adjusting to a change in your life. Doing something like brushing your teeth or eating with your non-dominant hand sets up new brain signals, and as you create the habit it becomes more automatic. It also slows you down and you may find an appreciation for that activity that you didn't have before. Gratitude is a habit that can help you during grief but it may not be the most natural habit to be in while you are in deep grief. Doing something like this introduces something new on a small scale, so you can adjust to it slowly as you begin to adjust to your loss.

Soul and Spirit

Grief is a soul experience. Your experience may have the effect of feeling like you are turning inside out, like your heart is breaking and you are losing parts of yourself. Each of us has in our deepest inner knowing the reality that death is the inevitable end game of our physical experience, whether a person or animal. While this may not bring immediate soothing of the shock or intensity of loss, it can provide an access to understanding that expands and informs the experience of grief. If you can hold the knowing that this is the nature of life, and be in your own experiences to express your grief, you will continue to move through your emotions. It is the re-identification of self in the loss that you must contend with and reestablish. The circumstances of the loss differ widely and the range of emotions may vary in intensity depending on the situation.

Things to soothe your soul include anything that invokes and uses your senses. If you consider that your body is in your soul, the body becomes the threshold of your soul's experience of the outer world. Think of it as creating a rhythm between your inner world and the outer environment. Isolating into inner thoughts and emotions that continue spiraling downward can be problematic and sink you into depression and anxiety. Medical intuitive Carol Ritberger, PhD maps grief to the lungs. She "sees" health problems begin at the level of the invisible, the subtle body, before they become manifest in the physical body. Take this opportunity to see that you can work with your grief in a way that helps you open to an expanded experience of yourself. There is more than this crushing pain you feel, and by surrendering to it enough to find expression in some way, you will learn something about yourself. You may find insights that would not otherwise be available to you as you work at this soul level of experience.

A woman named Lelani shared a wonderful project with me that helped her move through her grief. Spending fifteen minutes to one hour a day on her thirty-day project was very calming and meditative for her. Here are the steps she took in her creative work:

- She determined that she wanted to have a focal point each day and chose a word that represented what she was feeling and experiencing. There were ups and downs in her process and she allowed the word to be the start of her process for the day.

- Along with the word she chose each day, she did a drawing and added the Chinese character for the word in the top left corner of each page.

- Sharing the thirty-day project on Facebook created some social contact as well as accountability to do her work each day.

Throughout the years I have gathered a number of different exercises that have helped me express, accept, and move through difficult emotional experiences. Here are two that you may find helpful:

1. **Working With Clay:** Let your hands express what you are feeling by using clay or beeswax. If you have enough clay and/or beeswax, work with it for 7 days and save each piece you make so that at the end of 7 days you can look at the progression of shapes, of expression. You may find it helpful to hang on to some beeswax and keep it warmed in your hand as a way to soothe yourself, as well.

2. **The Four Elements Exercise**: (I'm grateful to my teacher Dennis Klocek at Rudolf Steiner College for this exercise.) The ancients believed that everything was made of four elements: Earth, Water, Air, and Fire. These were considered the energy forces that sustain life and all of them are integral parts of the physical universe. For this exercise we will be putting the elements in a circular path, a mandala. You will learn how to move with your emotions in a particular direction that leads to something hidden to you now.

   a) First, let's go back to the discussion of alchemy. Alchemy is the process of transforming something of a lower nature into a higher state through intense heat. As such, your pain is the fire. Another imagination is to see the experience you are

93

having as a crucible—place yourself in the crucible, and let this experience move in you with the understanding that your emotions are the fire that provides inner transformation. The four elements are a way of engaging in the experience with the idea of taking an emotion through its alchemical process with imagery and engaging with the images as they change for you.

b) To prepare for this exercise, gather an art pad or drawing tablet, crayons or colored pencils, scissors, glue, and some magazines that have images. You may also want to journal about your experience in each of the elements. It could also be helpful to have a partner who agrees to listen to you as you share what the images represent for you and anything else that you experience as you do this exercise. It can be done in one sitting, or over a period of days with reflection on your work each night before you go to bed.

c) Start with the element of Earth at the bottom of your page (you may want to have the orientation in landscape instead of portrait). Earth represents the facts, how you feel right now. Allow yourself to feel what you are feeling about your grief and begin to look at images in your magazines with the intent to find an image that represents this feeling in some way. Do not overthink this process. See what the image brings up in you to see if it matches what you are feeling. Cut this image, or images, out and glue them to the bottom of your page. Now pause and reflect on what you are sensing as you move your inner feeling into an outer expression.

d) Move clockwise to the left-hand side of the page. This is the Water element. For this image you are looking for something that represents how you feel now that you have taken the step to describe and depict how your grief and loss feel to you. Because you have taken this action, something has changed. This may be very subtle but ask yourself this question inwardly, "What has changed as a result of giving image to my feelings?" And pay attention to see if something arises. Is there a bit of light now? Did it become darker for you? Is there a particular color that seems to be emerging? Allow yourself to find images that say something about what has shifted.

e) At the top of the page is the element of Air. Air is the reversal of Earth. Carl Jung spoke of "enantiadromia," which is the movement of things to their opposite. The abundance of any force inevitably produces its opposite. Ask yourself, "If the opposite of how I feel in the Earth element were true, how would it appear?" What is the opposite of the image you found for Earth? This may be the most difficult one to do because the opposite of how you are feeling might not feel like something you can reach. I liken it to the dichotomy that so many people experience in which sadness and joy exist in the same moment over a memory. Do your best to work with the idea that grief is in movement, and working with your feelings in this way is creating movement in you. As you work with this, remember you do not need words to describe the state of Air, but allow yourself to look at images and imagine what the opposite of your Earth imagery might be.

f) At the right-hand side of the page is the element of Fire. With the Fire element you begin to get a glimpse of something that has remained hidden until now. You may have had an "aha" moment as you were moving through the process. If you had this experience, find an image that gives some meaning to the hidden thing or the "aha" that you experienced. If not, you can allow the Fire element to lie open and continue to work with it. Look at your mandala throughout the day and before you go to sleep. Sometimes you may need some time to go forwards and backwards through your images to let the process deepen inwardly for some hidden aspect, a thought, or a question that has been provoked.

These exercises allow you to access your emotions at a different level, and while this may all seem "woo-woo" to you, give it a go and see what happens! When you begin to work at this level, I can only facilitate and provide some structure for activity. Beyond this, it is your own individual and unique relationship with your grief that you are learning about and expressing.

Everything you need is within you. Continue to trust that you are in a process that is a shared human process. You are not alone in this, yet at the same time, in this moment it is your journey alone. This is another spiritual dichotomy and as you delve deeper into the human spiritual experience, you will find lessons often given through riddle and paradox. Trust yourself. Let yourself feel deeply and be human, using the fire of your emotions to engage in alchemy, to change something of lower nature into something higher. Seek wisdom.

Chapter 9

Paying Attention In Your Journey Forward

———— · ✦ · ————

I'm hoping that throughout this book you have recognized that you are not alone in your experience of grief and loss. While the inner work of moving through grief is done to some extent in aloneness, it is good to find a rhythm of moving in and out of solitude. There is a point at which isolation becomes a trigger to indulge in unhealthy behaviors. You need to stay alert to this. If you are taking action in some way in your aloneness and finding ways to express your grief, you will learn that when a memory or situation comes up that brings a pang of sadness, you can acknowledge it and just be with the emotions that are moving through you.

It's a Process

It is common to have experiences of grief hit you in waves. While this can be disarming, know that this is the nature of your emotions. I find the imagery of ocean waves, big and small, to be helpful. Gather imagery, poetry, websites, and groups that you can move in and out of as part of your "medicine bag" when you need tools at hand to quiet yourself, to let yourself cry, be angry, feel regret or whatever emotion is washing over you.

For myself, in my most recent experience with grief, memories from thirty years ago kept surfacing and making me very sad. I felt great regret about leaving my family all those years ago to live in a different state. My life away from them was based on a desire to live in a sunny climate but it also had something to do with wanting to grow up to some degree outside the family dynamic. I lived close enough to get home quickly if needed by plane, but far enough for the independence I felt I needed. While the family dynamic was always in play, I found that the distance I had given myself created the freedom to question some of the beliefs that were held in my family. It also allowed me to dive into experiences that brought the learning I needed as I continued on my spiritual path.

The regret that I was feeling came as a surprise to me and it definitely needed processing. I allowed myself to feel the regret but also to recognize the ways in which I did have a rich family life—love was an ever-present quality. Much of the processing that occurs in grief is around love, either how you expressed it, or how you withheld it, or how it was given or not given to you. The processing of this one quality is a lifetime of work! How many of us really experience unconditional love? How many of us can truly give it? These were the questions that continued to surface for me in the in between times of grief experiences when I was trying to adjust to loss. I found there were many shadow aspects of what I thought was a true expression of love. I remember being startled by my own realization that I had become very attached to a kind of possessive love for my little brother that excluded the possibility that anyone's suffering could be as bad as mine. This is very difficult for me to disclose because, of course, my mom and dad had great difficulty losing their youngest child. Of course his girlfriend of three years was devastated. Of course my brothers felt this loss too, but I had closed down in my experience and isolated myself in my grief.

What I am pointing to here is the need to pay attention to where your thoughts are going as your journey moves along. I found that I had enshrined my little brother Martin and that was hurting me. When I attended the Grief Recovery Method® I had already done lots of processing with this initial loss in my life, but I found there were still some unmet expectations and longings in me that I needed to work out, and it was this relationship that I worked with during my experience in the class. It was very freeing and I found the work so helpful that I am now certified to help people through this process.

In my spiritual striving I continue to learn about birth, death, and rebirth as a rhythmic occurrence. I know that the physical levels of relationships in my life are all time-bound, because as human beings that is the reality. It makes me much more open to people to find understanding of what I can learn about myself in the reflection of another. I look to a higher level in all my relationships to see if I can experience the understanding of why we have come together on a soul level.

Many years ago I read the book *Sacred Contracts* by Caroline Myss, which provided an expanded view of the soul qualities of relationships. The body of work that I did with medical intuitive Carol Ritberger in Egyptian Mysteries opened my mind and my heart to a much more expansive view of a higher order of life on Earth. When I then added Anthroposophy and the work with *Karmic Relationships*, I had a much greater capacity for understanding and experiencing loss in a different way. All of this spiritual understanding brought new meaning to the pain and struggle I was experiencing. I purify a part of myself when I allow myself to experience the emotions. It is also a way in which I can build a greater quality of empathy. I think that this life is meant for building capacities of love, compassion, and empathy. Sometimes your greatest struggle through pain may open up to your offering to another as the *wounded healer*.

When I spoke to Tom about his feeling that he needed somewhere for his love to go after he lost his wife, I realized that much of the pain of loss is in having love to give that is not being received. This part of you that gave this love is looking for a place to continue giving it. I believe this is why my own deep healing this past year came when I found a way to focus this part of me that wanted to give of myself. Many people I spoke with talked about finding ways to serve others and how that felt healing to them. Tom's comment awakened a truth I had not seen, that was unnamed in me. This is the gift of finding ways and places to share your grief. We are awakened in each other's suffering as well as in our capacity to love.

Creating Accountability

I recognized for myself last year that I had so much love to give and now there were fewer people who were receiving it. Most of my family was gone, I had no children, and my remaining family lived in other states. I thought that I had put enough things into place for myself that I was fine and I could handle my grief process as it continued. I was wrong, however, and didn't recognize that I was underwater until I went to a conference in the summer that I have been going to for years. It was a safe haven of friends, people who had known me through the years, people who supported me in my grief. My withdrawn state during the conference worried me but I could not seem to engage with people in the way I usually did. What I had not seen for myself was that I needed to create some accountability for my continued movement forward.

There were several presenters who spoke on topics related to positive psychology and the science of happiness. I decided that I needed to take on my own Happiness Project with an N=1 (me). I stood on a stage and shared that as a wellness professional I had not seen how at risk I was in my own journey and that I was slipping below the waterline. I made a plea to the audience to pay attention to where we might create services to support people just like me in our workplaces. I also let them know that I was taking on my own Happiness Project, which had three criteria: nurturing social relationships, showing acts of kindness, and expressing gratitude. I gave them my email address and invited them to contact me anytime during the year to check in on me. Several did and it was a helpful reminder to be consistent with my efforts.

Turning Outward

That moment of taking responsibility for my state of being, for my chronic state of unhappiness, changed me. I am so grateful for my colleague Joel who invited me to stand on that stage and share my wellness story. It was a soul retrieval—I called back a part of myself that day that was becoming lost to me out of sharing my vulnerability.

Pay attention and be grateful for those people who come into your life and provide an opportunity to move forward!

I turned outward in that moment and it was the beginning of the quest to find that state called "joy" or "happy" again. Those two words had become a distant memory and this was deeply disturbing because most who know me know that I am the one who brings the "happy." I felt like grief had finally changed my personality and I didn't know if I would find myself again. It felt as if all I could see were memories of loss—losing two dear friends to suicide, my little brother to leukemia, my cousin in a house fire, my running buddy in the birth of her first child, my mom, my dad, and my older brother—it was all too much. The totality of all these losses was pressing in on me and "happy" was completely out of reach and I had no idea how I would bring it back, or if I *could* bring it back.

When I left the conference I turned my efforts outward and looked for opportunities to serve others. This was the turning point for me and this book is one of my efforts from that decision to turn outward in service. In speaking with many of the individuals for this book, many shared that turning outwards in service was also an important step in their recovery process through grief and adjusting to loss in their life.

As I shared earlier in this book, another step for me was a moment where I was sitting on my couch consumed in sadness when I decided I did not want to feel that way anymore—I chose joy. Joy seemed like a leap from happiness, but in that moment it was what came to me. As I continued on my path to recovery, one day I realized the paradox of being able to hold joy and sadness in the same moment. Others shared a dichotomy like this with me, too. I believe it is one of the mysteries of being human and having the capacity to experience the range of emotions that are part of our humanity.

Creating Community in New Experiences

You may find yourself seeking out new experiences in this turning outward. Many are pushed to ask some universal questions that most people ask at some time in their life. "Who am I?" and "Why am I here?" These questions may move you to explore new experiences to find answers.

Searching out opportunities that offer a different cultural experience and teaching can be helpful. I found that my faith as well as multiple perspectives from other teachings broadened my ability to be with my grief. For many years I was part of a shamanic healing community. Experiences like a grief circle and a "Spirit Canoe" can be very rich experiences if you are open to seeking a spiritual experience of grief that supports you in this world but also connects to the realm of Spirit. I also found the ceremony and rituals of my family's faith, Catholicism, comforting in some ways as I participated with my family. I learned about the traditions in the Hebrew faith around death and dying and the support through the grieving process to be affirming and loving. Find what your heart is seeking in experience and learning. Ultimately it is the expression of love that is the counterpart of grief. There are myriad opportunities to learn about yourself as a loving being.

Chapter 10

Remembering and Moving Forward

As you continue to move forward in your days, months, years and to adjust to your loss, the depth of emotional sadness may begin to lessen. If it does not to any degree and you find that you cannot engage with life in a meaningful way, it may be time to seek some additional help. It's important to continue to care for yourself and your adjustment to loss. The important thing to remember is that it is a process and taking action in time will move you forward—time itself will not heal.

Backslide

"I can't let go because I don't want to forget." I've heard this often from people, this fear of forgetting. Part of the problem with this is that you can get yourself into a habit of immortalizing and aggrandizing the person you do not want to forget. There are a couple of ways to help yourself with this fear of forgetting.

Keeping a small altar of sorts for your loved one can be comforting, but I also add the step of checking in with yourself from time to time to see if you have become attached to the things you have placed on your remembrance altar. I had an area for my little brother that included a picture of him when we were on a trip to France together, and a music box with the song Camelot. My brother and I had enjoyed long philosophical conversations as we both moved into our adulthood and he had become my best friend. Even while enjoying a loving relationship with someone, I did not share those kinds of conversations with anyone but my brother. I missed him terribly for a long time and each time I played that music box I became deeply sad about what could have been and never would be in our relationship as we grew older together. When I looked at the picture, on the other hand, I had feelings of happiness that we had gone to France together. I recognized that if I wanted to stop going into that deep well of sadness the music box evoked, I needed to stop engaging with it. It sounds like such a simple thing but this is the type of recognition that is important to have as you are moving through grief. It is natural and normal to feel sad, but this was a couple years later that sadness overwhelmed me. I recognized I needed to stop and I took the music box out of the house at about 3am in the morning one sleepless night. This was a step in my recovery.

During the writing of this book, I was doing some major cleaning and clearing after coming back from a family visit in which we were throwing and sorting some of my mom and dad's things that had been stored at my brother Michael's house. I had the feeling when I got home that I didn't want people to have to do all that hard work of sorting and throwing out my stuff when I die. I have since purged many things from my closets and feel lighter in not being attached to so many things.

Another way to keep the memory alive of your lost loved one is to simply allow conversation to flow in a way that makes everyone around you recognize that it's okay to talk about. When you have the freedom to speak of memories both good and sad, you are normalizing your grief experience for others. This is healthy for everyone concerned.

Complicated Grief

Practitioners have recognized that about 10% of people become entrenched in grief in such a way that they cannot move forward in their life. If you find that after about a year you are still entrenched in deep grief and are still having trouble functioning in everyday activities, it may be time to seek professional help. Some other symptoms include:

- Focusing on little else but your loved one's death

- Extreme focus on reminders of the loved one or excessive avoidance of reminders

- Intense and persistent longing or pining for the deceased

- Problems accepting the death

- Numbness or detachment

- Bitterness about your loss

- Feeling that life holds no meaning or purpose

- Lack of trust in others

- Inability to enjoy life or think back on positive experiences with your loved one

Remember there are many emotions you might experience in grief, such as anger, regret, and numbness. Different people follow different paths through the grieving experience. Allowing yourself to experience the pain of your loss is part of being able to move through it. Adjusting to a new reality and accepting that the loss has happened occurs over time.

Compound Effect of Grief

Several people I interviewed shared with me that it was a

compounding effect of several deaths over a relatively short period of time that made it so difficult to process. I would put myself in the same category. Part of what happened in the seven-year period in which I lost my mom, dad, and brother was also compounded by changing identities as these years moved along. I went from being the child to parenting my parents in some small ways.

As I mentioned in the last chapter, adjusting to the loss of most of my family was overwhelming. I was revisiting memories from my childhood and then into my twenties when I moved away from my family to California. I revisited places I'd frequented and even took a tour of the high-rise apartment I lived in when I was twenty-four and many of my family members had visited. After I let myself feel the sadness I found a strength welling up in me. I was very strong and independent in those days and felt very weakened from the past few years of loss. Feeling my aloneness often made me feel helpless in the first stages of my grief recovery. Now when I notice myself heading toward that loneliness, I reach out and connect in some way to the people in my life who love me and are part of my community.

Almost a year after my older brother died (as I'm finishing the writing of this book), my sister-in-law stopped breathing and was put on a ventilator. I went into overdrive with worry and concern for not only her but the other family members and how they were being affected. The level of fear in my body was intense and I felt like I had completely slid back into the kind of grief that would engulf me, rendering me unable to deal with life and work. While I did have a few days of extreme reaction, I had support at work and I put all of my habits that kept my body healthy with all the stress in full swing to keep me on an even keel. Being a trainer and coach with HeartMath®, these techniques are the first line of defense for me in connecting to my heart and not letting my head thoughts lead me down a dark alley. They help balance the physiology of stress I'm experiencing in my body.

My sister-in-law recovered and I recognized that I was still in a state of recovery and continue to work with grief for myself and the part of myself that went into such an extreme reaction. It's important that you have your tools ready (social support, self-care, etc.) so you are prepared to help yourself. A low-level anxiety may be present that can get triggered easily as you are continuing to move forward. This is part of a natural and normal process as your heart, mind, and body are all moving back to balance.

Spiritual Help, Affirmations, and Actions for Hard Times

One of the habits I used to fall back into to disconnect and stop feeling was drinking red wine at night and on the weekends. I recall one time when I decided drinking alcohol was just making things worse—it is a depressant after all. I had taken to the habit of just lying around in bed and wallowing. While I was feeling despondent I was also calling out to the universe for help. There are many different ways that the spiritual world opens in response to a plea. People share different ways that synchronicity and divine intervention are part of their experience. This particular time for me was pretty interesting and helpful.

As I was lying there unable to find any particular reason to climb out of bed I went into a meditative state and began to see an octopus start wrapping his arms around me in a way that was holding on to me just tightly enough to bring me up through the water to the surface. When my head came out of the water's surface and I felt the sun on my face, I found enough energy in me to get up out of bed, put my tennis shoes on, and go out and walk by the river. Then I was ready to go to the social gathering that was on my calendar that day. The octopus became a symbol for me and occasionally I would be out and see a stuffed octopus, a glass one at Home Goods, or a photograph in a museum. I had never paid much attention to octopuses before but it was such a compelling experience that I could just think about it and I would choose to get my butt out of bed! Ask for help—who knows who will show up for you? Of course, I say that with deepest honor for all spiritual traditions and for myself. Archangel Michael is never far away in my thoughts and prayers when I ask for strength. Rely on your spiritual practices if you have them—the spiritual world is just waiting for us to ask for guidance!

As I stated earlier, I see Spirit within and behind all things, and so I accepted this experience easily and thanked the spiritual world for meeting me in my need. You may not have had this kind of experience, but I would offer to you that moments of crisis in your life are often a call from Spirit to begin seeing your life, your being, and your consciousness in an expanded way. The gift of moving through pain is wisdom. The wisdom I learned that day was "I am not alone." This has been a theme in my life that repeats and repeats and repeats itself in different ways. You may find that in your struggle through grief you recognize a theme. While I would never wish on anyone the kind of pain I have endured at times, I've also seen that struggle is the way in which growth happens. Moving through, transforming, and transcending the pain of grief and loss opens up to something new and unexpected, but you cannot see it until you allow yourself to grieve.

When you have those particularly hard days or times, find some words or inspirations that help you recognize you are "in it." In the realm of alchemy you could use the picture of the crucible. You are in the fire purifying and in the ash that will be left is the seed for something new, a rebirth of some kind out of this experience.

One of the simplest affirmations I used when I was in depression and stuck in the mud of grief was, "This sucks! While I'm here I might as well look around." That may not sound like an affirmation but it helped me make a choice to not wallow but be curious. If you can see yourself

116

choosing in some way in all the darkness, something will change, something will move, and something will be made known to you. Remember, something in you is dying; a part of you is ready to go in order to birth something new in you. You may need to keep repeating this process. I know for myself I would probably have been diagnosed as clinically depressed during a couple of the years in this past decade, because the days dragged on and on into months and months and then years. But I was too stubborn to go to a doctor to get a diagnosis, nor did I think it would help to be prescribed medication to deal with it. I'm so sensitive to medications I just didn't see that direction going well for me. I stayed in the mud and the muck of what I was feeling, kept lifting one heavy foot after another, knowing that I was moving forward, and it kept being dark, and it kept being hard, but I knew this was just a part of the experience. I also had a healing community that knew where I was in my process. I was known.

A wise friend and colleague of mine, Brenda Gustin of Union with Heart, has this sage mantra: "Don't force life; flow with your Life Force." I encourage you to find different ways to feel the chi, prana, or life force in your body move. Mantak Chia has some fantastic books that teach you how to meditate and move the different circuitries of energy in your body. If you can find a Tai Chi or Qigong class to join, you will have the social component, which is very helpful. All emotions have an energetic component of movement flow in your life.

Finding a New Normal

From time to time the cloud of sadness may fall over you again. There are different triggers that might make this happen. If you know of particular times that feel like they may be hard, draw support around you. Plan to honor your loss in some way on that day and be with people.

The road to finding a new normal happens with each baby step you take in your grief recovery. An incomplete past with your grief may set you up for a difficult future. There is no timetable for finding a new normal. You will know you have moved into this state when your loss becomes a part of the story of you, when you can speak easily of memories, when you can be sad from time to time and express these feelings, and when you feel safe and trusting in new relationships.

Keeping busy, as many people advise those in grief, can be a double-edged sword. It can set you up in a pattern of what I call "overdrive." It's fine to be getting back to your own goals and business but not if it's to the exclusion of grieving your loss. I have often used this tactic and been thrown back into a deep, overwhelming loss of energy and emotional stability. It's like my body knows better now and I've learned to listen!

Be strong. How much stronger would our children be if they saw that a range of emotions is normal and accepted? There are many adults I've spoken with who said that as a child they were shielded from grief, and through this experience they learned that sad feelings should be hidden or experienced alone. Some of my most healing moments have come from being with a coworker who just let me cry in the middle of the day. She was just there for me like a witness to my grief for a moment and then I was clear and able to get on with my workday. Those who have experienced a loss and grieved in a healthy way can be with you and allow you to express yours.

When you begin to feel happy, accept that happiness. Many feel guilty and keep themselves attached to some expectation (either internally or externally) to having to be in a morbid state.

Learn who the people are in your life that you can talk to about the good and the bad things as you move along. Find those experiences that take you into the world of experience and let you stay in touch with your grief in order to feel it. Many people find at a particular point that a creative activity becomes a healing tool. The idea is not to dwell in the feelings but to express them. This is why creative outlets often help move you forward. They are a way your soul can find expression; you are creating, bringing life to something.

Conclusion

Transformed Pain

——— · ✦ · ———

Throughout my experiences with grief in my life, I feel I have taken on the hero's journey, a concept out of the work of Joseph Campbell that symbolizes man's inner desire to overcome his darkest troubles and emerge victorious. Upon the return in this journey, the hero lives with wisdom throughout the rest of his life. This journey requires the steps through struggle for psychological wholeness (termed "Individuation" by Carl Jung). I have always felt the desperate need to understand death, this thing that comes to all of us but is feared by most of us. I have learned as a spiritual seeker that as I continue to grow and learn in the unfolding of my life, staying open to new levels of wisdom is beneficial. That being said, I feel I have learned much about death and consider it a topic to continue learning about in my own inner work as well as with others. This is where the Death Café gatherings are doing a great service. I think if we more openly discuss death, we will be able to live more completely in our life!

What's Possible?

Now, when I think of F Ground 37 (my little brother Martin's hospital room), I think of love. What an incredible outpouring from people I didn't know and people I did, including myself. I did not know the capacity for love I had before I went through the experience of my brother being diagnosed with Acute Myelogenous Leukemia and dying two and a half months later. Months after Martin died, I visited the hospital so that I could talk with all the nurses and social workers who had tended my brother and family during those two and a half months. I stood in F Ground 37 again and wrote in my journal, "I wish only to feel that love again and realize it's within when I remember that it was me who gave so much and thought so little about why, and love was all there was. So much happened in here and yet it's not as traumatic being in here as I thought it would be. Perhaps it is as it should be—felt, experienced, and learned from and put away to allow for new things in life to arrive."

When my little brother's ten-year reunion came around a few months after his passing, I wrote a letter for his class and prepared some pictures of his life. In it I wrote, "Although Martin's death has torn my family's hearts open, we have all learned a powerful love in allowing ourselves to open to the pain. Somehow the wonder and grace of all that Martin taught us as we cared for him sustains and helps us see that death really is the other half of life."

One of the greatest gifts of being with my big brother Michael through his treatment and death was the immense amount of unconditional love I felt for him and his process. I was so agitated at some points, wanting to talk about death and how he was feeling and completing things with him. To his dying breath he thought he'd get better and did everything he could with treatment and never gave in. I had to step so far back from what I wanted and what my expectations were and just sit beside him on his bed and watch TV with him and know how much this meant to him when I visited. His family did the same—just loved him to the end.

I am bigger in my ability to be empathetic; I am a bigger vessel of love. I am a wounded healer. I can see all of this in the big picture now. When you are in the pain and muck and chaos it's hard to see the writing of the epic novel of your life, but trust that your whole life matters and that your book of life is being written by you, and pain and struggle are vehicles to purify something in you.

If you picked up this book it may have been for the purpose of learning something that can help you work through your grief. You may also have been drawn to it without really understanding why you were drawn to it. I hope you have picked up a thought or two that will move you to some action in your life. You will hear your soul's voice when you continue to press forward, and pressing forward may mean finally letting yourself feel what you have not wanted to feel.

Some Statistics

For some, grief may be triggered and arise strongly from decades of pushing it away, denying it, or just thinking that you should "get over it." Being able to experience grief fully is a human birthright. I attempt more and more to live in such a way that I celebrate everything, knowing that change is constant and that all things living are moving toward a death of some kind.

I am an avid follower of the work of Kelly Brogan, MD, whose views on suicidality I mentioned earlier. Here are some of the statistics and information she provides that I find concerning:

- 11% of Americans are on psychiatric medicine for depression

- 1 in 4 of reproductive age are taking an anti-anxiety or anti-depressant

- Depression is the #1 cause of disability according to WHO (World Health Organization) worldwide— our treatments are not diminishing the suffering

Unresolved grief can become a hidden seed for future unrest like depression. If you picked up this book because you have some sense of something lost, I encourage you to find avenues to question with curiosity what you are experiencing. Find support and a safe space to do this. When I worked as a shamanic healer, one of the most profound experiences I witnessed was assisting another with a return of a soul "part" that had fractured in some kind of trauma. I work in different ways now to help people uncover and heal parts of themselves that were denied the experience of grief. For some this may feel completely confronting. While it may be that doing the inner work and moving through seems daunting, the freedom and beauty on the other side is life giving.

The possibility of learning about yourself as a loving being is what lies behind the intense experience of loss. This journal excerpt I wrote when I was thirty-one, just months after my little brother Martin died, set the stage for how I would handle the many losses to come over the next twenty-five years: "To sit and feel the pain again is hard and yet through the greatest pain has come the greatest love in my life. As we cleared away his (Martin's) belongings I felt how temporary everything seemed, but not the love. It endures and can't be put away. And so I try to go on with all of it and remember that all of me except the love is also temporary."

I encourage you to look into your life to see if unresolved grief has affected your ability to live a life fully alive. While the old saying goes—time heals—in my experience unless you are doing something in that time to experience the feelings you may be wanting to push away, they are storing up in you in ways that may present as fear in new relationships, loss of strength to engage in new things, and physical health symptoms related to the storage of negative emotions in the cells of your body. The pioneering work of Candace Pert shows us that neuropeptides for emotions are found all over in the body's tissues. Is it possible that some of what you experience as physical pain has its origin in some sense of loss in your life?

There are many paths to moving through grief in a healthy way and finding avenues to recovery if you have buried yourself along with your loved one. That is how I felt one day when I realized how I was living my life years into my journey with my little brother's death—I was buried right there alongside him. Having recognized that it was one way to do grief, I am now more equipped and aware of the normal human process of grief and I have a much greater ability to let the process unfold and know that I will make it through. If you would like some help in moving through a process with your grief, please visit www.EnergyM.org.

As I reflect on all of the conversations I had in preparation for writing this book, as well as the hundreds of people I've worked with as a spiritual healer, I am profoundly struck by the courage and strength that people are capable of in confronting difficulty. I am also humbled in my own journey to reach this place of contribution as the wounded healer. I honor your journey and know that wisdom will be yours as you allow yourself to move in the mystery of human emotion to find what lies *in the experience* of grief, as well as what awaits on the other side.

About the Author

Michele Mariscal is a speaker, skilled facilitator and grief specialist. She combines her background in health, wellness, and spiritual development and healing to help individuals find greater meaning and movement forward in their life.

To contact Michele:

Call (916) 402-6188

Email at info@energym.org

Or visit her website www.EnergyM.org

Made in the USA
Coppell, TX
22 May 2023

17132760R00075